SAINTLY FEASTS
FOOD FOR SAINTS AND SCHOLARS

MARTINA MAHER & COLETTE SCULLY

Saints selected by
DRIES VAN DEN AKKER SJ
with assistance from
JOE MUNITIZ SJ

Moving blur in the dining room at Manresa.

First published 2019 by Messenger Publications

ISBN: 978 1 78812 027 2

Manresa Novitiate & Author Photography: Paula T Nolan
Food Photography: Shutterstock.com
Graphics of Saints: Messenger Publications

Designed by Messenger Publications Design Department
Typeset in Town 10 and Town 80
Printed by Halcyon Print Management Ltd

Messenger Publications,
37 Lower Leeson Street, Dublin 2
www.messenger.ie

Jesuit Refugee Service UK

The Jesuit Refugee Service (JRS) is an international Catholic organisation with a mission to accompany, serve as companions, and advocate for the rights of refugees and forcibly displaced individuals worldwide. JRS in the UK has always held a special ministry to support those who find themselves held indefinitely in immigration detention, and those who have been left destitute by the asylum system in the UK. The work of JRS is informed by our core values and inspired by our faith in God who is present in human history, even in the most tragic moments.

Every day we encounter individuals who have experienced the indignity of destitution and detention. With no recourse to public funds, the refugees we serve are entirely reliant on the kindness and generosity of others to meet their basic needs. By walking alongside refugees and those seeking asylum we come to know personally those we serve and build lasting relationships with them.

Through our weekly Day Centre, we are able to provide a warm and welcoming environment for destitute refugees, offering practical support such as travel grants and toiletry packs. Alongside the Day Centre, JRS UK runs a number of activities that enable refugees to build confidence and resilience. We also run a small hosting scheme, providing short-term, stable accommodation for those we accompany who would otherwise be homeless.

We are able to offer emotional support and social visits to those in detention, a very isolating and uncertain situation. As part of our commitment to walk alongside those we serve, we continue to raise the issue of their mistreatment and advocate for change.

By attending to practical and emotional needs, JRS UK seeks to provide a counter culture in a time of continuing hostility to refugees and forcibly displaced persons.

JRS UK, 2 Chandler Street, London, E1W 2QT
020 7488 7310 | uk@jrs.net | www.jrsuk.net

Facebook: /jesuitrefugeeserviceuk
Twitter: @JRSUK

You can help JRS welcome refugees with dignity and compassion. Your donation will support JRS UK to accompany destitute and detained refugees in a spirit of hospitality, welcome and love.
Find out how to donate by visiting www.jrsuk.net/donate

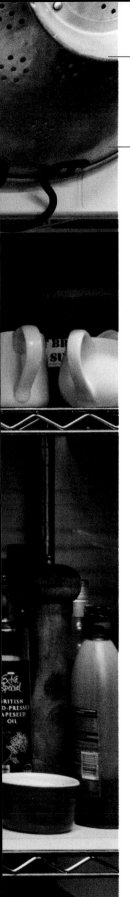

CONTENTS

Manresa Novitiate, Birmingham.

MANRESA, BIRMINGHAM

MEET THE PLACE

SHORT HISTORY OF MANRESA NOVITIATE IN BIRMINGHAM

From 1912 to 1918 the Sisters of Mercy conducted a convent school on the premises. They named it Saint Gabriel's, after the Italian Gabriele Possenti dell'Addolorata, a seminarian of the Passionist Order, who died at the age of 24 in 1862. He was beatified in 1908 as an example for young people, and canonised in 1920. The naming of the house was probably inspired by the Passionist community who were responsible for the local parish. After 1918 the school was directed by the Sisters of the Holy Child.

RETREAT CENTRE OF SAINT GABRIEL

In 1938 the Archdiocese of Birmingham bought the house for £4,580, and enlarged it at a cost of £7,000 to make it a retreat house for men of the Archdiocese. The old hall was adapted to the needs of a retreat house. Out-houses were demolished and a new three-storey bedroom block was added. The Jesuits took over in 1978 and it became a novitiate.

THE MISSION OF MANRESA HOUSE, HARBORNE, BIRMINGHAM

In a world of division and deafness, how can we open our eyes and ears to one another, to the cries of the poor, and the groaning of the earth? How can we act with freedom, boldness, enthusiasm, fervour and compassion in reaching out to others, bringing healing, consolation and reconciliation to the estranged? As Pope Francis has exhorted: 'we need to be artisans of peace, for building peace is a craft that demands serenity, creativity, sensitivity and skill'. (*Rejoice and Be Glad*, 89)

Manresa House aims to form people in this way: artisans of peace and unity, who act from a place of depth and contemplation. Thus, the purpose of the house is to provide an environment for growth, just as Manresa in Spain was the place where the founder of the Jesuits, Saint Ignatius of Loyola, grew in the life of God and himself became an artisan of peace, unity and consolation. Manresa was the '... mystical cave which witnessed the successive agents of his great spirit: from the serene peace of the beginner to the purifications of the dark night of the soul, and finally to the mystical graces of the visions of the Trinity'. (Paul VI, to the 32nd General Congregation)

Similarly, Manresa House in Harborne, Birmingham, aims to be a place where Jesuit novices grow in the life of the Spirit. They become able to discern the promptings of God and so to recognise the darkest and brightest elements in ourselves and in our world. It is a place where novices practise and grow in the virtues of prudence, temperance, justice and courage, as well as the theological virtues of faith, hope and charity. It is a place of safety and sanctuary, but also one of struggle and wilderness, both preparing and initiating its inhabitants for a life of complete surrender to God and service to the world.

April 2019

SAINT IGNATIUS AS COOK

With this book we give honour to a not often remembered aspect of Saint Ignatius' way of doing, recalled in his first biography by Father Petrus Ribadineira SJ [219.9].

After assuming the office of general superior, Ignatius began in earnest to establish the details pertaining to his administration of the entire Society, as well as those pertaining to the order of its community life. Wanting the modesty of his behaviour to match with the height to which he had risen, and wanting his example to challenge everyone else to a zeal for genuine humility, he at once went into the kitchen and there, for a good length of time, he took on the role of cook.

He also undertook other common household chores so conscientiously and earnestly that he looked like some novice acting purely for the sake of self-improvement. Since, in the midst of the very important items of business that kept coming up for for him every day, he could not be freely and fully available for such duties, he so divided his time that he attended to the more serious matters without neglecting the kitchen.

APERITIF

'... and don't forget hospitality,
for by doing this, some people have entertained angels without knowing it.'
(Letter to the Hebrews 13:2)

When, in the 1560s, the Society of Jesus asked novices what it was that attracted them to this way of life, their answers were striking: they noticed in Jesuits and in Jesuit communities, *'hilaritas, elegantia morum, suavitas'* ('cheerfulness, graciousness and an ease to be with') (John O'Malley SJ, *The First Jesuits*, p. 55). Anyone who has had the pleasure of enjoying Sunday lunch in Manresa House prepared by Colette and Martina will know what these novices meant.

On 1 August 2017, Manresa House celebrated forty years as a novitiate, and in October 2017, Colette and Martina celebrated twenty-two uninterrupted years of preparing the Sunday lunches as well as the feasts at the celebration of first vows of novices. A happy coincidence of years as Martina, born on 29 February 1928, was also celebrating her twenty-second birthday, there being only twenty-two leap years since her birth! On 1 March 2018, Martina celebrated her ninetieth birthday – one week later, Colette celebrated her seventy-fifth! *Saintly Feasts* is, then, one way of saying 'thank you' to both Colette and Martina for their 'cheerfulness, graciousness and ease to be with' as they have welcomed and fed, at so many levels, the novices, the Jesuit community and friends of Manresa House.

The hope is that these recipes will help us not only 'to savour and relish'– as Saint Ignatius encourages us to do in the Spiritual Exercises (second annotation) – the meals we have enjoyed at the hands of Colette and Martina, but also to help future Jesuits and friends of the Society of Jesus to continue welcoming and feeding those searching for their true homeland, especially those strangers in our land, 'migrants and refugees, men and women in search of peace' (Pope Francis' message for Peace and Justice Sunday 2018).

The recipes are arranged in sections – Soup & Starters, Fish, Meat, Vegetables etc. – as listed in the Menu. However, a Calendar Index also lists them following the liturgical year, and there is an alphabetical list of the names of the saints.

Finally, a word of deep gratitude to Dries van den Akker SJ and Joe Munitiz SJ (current and previous members of the Manresa House community). They first chose the saints and together wrote up a text for each one. Novices have been a great help in typing up the recipes, borrowed from a variety of sources, but all adapted (and tasted with approval). And last but not least, a word of thanks to Gill Clack who, with patient and loving attention, did all the correction work. Our hope is that a book prepared with such love will be in itself a feast to behold. Thank you!

Fr Simon Bishop SJ
Director of Novices

Martina and Colette in the kitchen at Manresa.

29 FEBRUARY 2018
ON THE OCCASION OF MARTINA'S 90th BIRTHDAY
FOR MARTINA (& COLETTE)

Melody 'Devoted to You' (Everly Brothers)

all your cooking every dish
salmon, sea bream: every fish
we're all by your Irish stew
devoted to you

roast beef, chicken, pheasant and steaks
breads and scones and pies and cakes
we're by every course you do
devoted to you

recipes either cold or warm
where did you learn all this?
you learned it all at home on the farm
which for all here a blessing is.

mousse and soup and legs of the lamb
sweet courgettes and gammon and ham
we're by your potatoes too
devoted to you

your desserts and heavenly scones
and the drumsticks with their bones
all your cooking we went through:
!!!DEVOTED TO YOU!!!

Composed by Dries van den Akker SJ

COLETTE SCULLY

MARTINA MAHER

I grew up on the north side of Dublin city. My dad would have liked to be an architect, but due to sad circumstances he was unable to achieve his goal. His father died leaving his wife and children with very little money for education. He had to take up work as a joiner at a very young age, to support the family. He made all the furniture in our home, which was of a very high standard. He never really achieved what he was interested in.

Dries van den Akker, pictured below, is a Dutch Jesuit living in Manresa Novitiate in Birmingham. Dries researched and wrote the text on the saints best connected to each recipe. See page 22.

I was born into a farming family in Tipperary. We grew everything that was needed in the kitchen for every meal. Wheat to make soda bread and other breads, and porridge. Milk came from our herd of cows. Some went to the local creamery to make butter and whipping cream. When all the cream was extracted from the milk you brought it back home to separate in your churn. After a couple of hours, the milk thickened, and you had natural yogurt, which was used in making the bread. We drank it from the churn. Some girls washed their faces with it to keep their skin fresh and lovely. The young calves enjoyed it and the pigs found it refreshing on a warm day.

DRIES VAN DEN AKKER SJ

INTERVIEWING THE AUTHORS

On Friday, 7 December 2018, **Paula Nolan** from Messenger Publications met for a chat with Martina (left above) and Colette, the authors of *Saintly Feasts*.

How did it come about that the two of you started cooking Sunday dinners for the Jesuit Novitiate at Manresa?

Martina: Well, one day I was in the kitchen at Manresa with Paddy [Fr Patrick Purnell SJ] and he was saying they needed someone to cook Sunday dinner. I said we'd do it, but he said no, that wouldn't be right at all, but could I ask around if anyone would be able to take it on. I said, 'No, I won't. People should be at home with their families on a Sunday.' So in the end he agreed we'd do it for four Sundays, and then we'd see if they were happy, and if we were happy, with the arrangement. Well, we never talked about it again!

Colette: You see, we were coming here when it was Saint Gabriel's Retreat House, a long time before we started cooking. When the cooking came about, Martina had just retired from work with Social Services, and I could work in my nursing and have Sundays off. I'm all the better that they let me do the Sunday lunches.

Where did your love of cooking come from?

Colette: Here! It came from cooking here! Before that we'd make dinners for ourselves, of course, but nothing fancy. It was when we started cooking here for a whole lot of people that we would try out different recipes. We had a system whereby one week we'd have lamb, another chicken, another beef, another fish, and we'd have different starters and desserts. If the dinner was heavy, we'd just have soup to start, or a light starter. We'd get feedback from the novices: what did they think of them? So we could experiment. Then, on special occasions like birthdays and Vow Days, we'd make cakes.

Martina: We would make lots of different desserts. We'd make our own custard, and even our own ice cream, and this was before the ice cream-making machines. We made pies and tarts and puddings.

Colette: We made Bakewell Tarts. Did you know that Bakewell Tarts have a secret ingredient? The original Bakewell has a flavour like no other. It's probably an essence of some sort. I do know some people use ground rice instead of ground almonds, but we don't. The almond flavour is an important part of a good Bakewell.

So you cooked on other occasions as well?

Colette: On Vow Days, we would cook for up to one hundred people. Depending on how many were taking their vows. If there were only a few, they'd have the ceremony in the Chapel at Manresa, and then come straight downstairs to the dining room. But if there were so many taking vows that they wouldn't fit in the Chapel, the ceremony was in nearby Saint Mary's Church. The novice master would say at the end of the vow ceremony, 'You are all welcome to come back to Manresa for lunch', and there could be well over a hundred in the Church. But they wouldn't all come down.

Martina: We used to put together two long tables, one on either side of the door to the garden. On the first table we'd make a spread of plates of food to self-serve, and on the other table, the exact same food, a replica. Then at the end of the room, a table with cakes and desserts. People could eat standing, or sit on chairs we put around the place, or sit outside. We never used paper plates!

Colette: Vow Days are major occasions. They were a lot of work but they were wonderful. We have seen a lot of novices go through their training here over the years. We knew Simon (current novice master) from when he was here as a novice.

What have you most enjoyed about cooking at Manresa every Sunday?

Colette: The company. It's great company. And the people. We've met so many people over the twenty-two years, and made so many friends. This year we have sent one hundred and twenty Christmas cards to people we met here and their families, because we got to know some of the families too.

Did you do the food shopping for Sunday dinner?

Martina: Yes. We used to go to Asda every week and we'd go around with two trolleys, one for ourselves, and one for Manresa. And even though we knew nobody expected us to penny-pinch, we had our own rule never to spend more than £5 a head.

Colette: There was a man at the till and he started asking us what we were doing with the two trolleys, so we explained to him, and we told him about the cakes we'd make for birthdays and Vow Days at Manresa. Well, didn't he ask us to make a birthday cake for his daughter, and we became great friends. So by doing the cooking here we have made other friends outside Manresa.

So would you say that cooking here on Sundays changed your lives?

Colette: Oh definitely. Like I said, we have made such good friends. Gerry (Fr Gerry Marsden SJ), who was here when we started cooking, moved to Glasgow, and we kept in touch over all the years and the two of us were at his bedside when he died. He was very good to us.

Martina: At one stage we didn't have any holidays for a few years, except we would go to Glasgow for a few days to see Gerry. So the people we met through cooking at Manresa definitely changed our lives and became lifelong friends.

What are the meals you have found are the favourites?

Colette: I suppose they loved our cheese soufflé. Yes, that was very popular. But we never told them what we were going to cook on Sunday. It was always a surprise. On a Wednesday, we'd take down some of our cookbooks from the shelf, and decide what we'd do for starter, main course and dessert. And from that we'd make our shopping list.

Martina: Oh, and they loved our Yorkshire Pudding! We'd make it in the huge big roasting dish, and when it was ready the novice master would clink his glass for silence so everybody would watch us bring it in to the table, and that way nobody missed seeing it risen, because the minute you put a knife in it, down it went!

Colette: And they loved our summer pudding.

Did any of the Jesuits take up cooking?

Colette: Well we have to mention Stephen (Stephen Noon SJ). For our last two years cooking Sunday dinners, he helped us. He would take the heavy roast dishes out of the oven for us, as well as join us in preparing the meals, and he was a great help.

Have you seen things change much in the novitiate?

Martina: We've been coming here from the very

Cookbook library at Colette and Martina's home.

beginning, and the main changes have been that each new novice master has his own style. But it's always been a welcoming place. That has never changed over the years.

What do you miss most about your Sundays cooking here at the novitiate?

Colette: Coming out of Mass at nine o'clock on a Sunday morning. For twenty-two years after Mass we'd come straight here and start the dinner. Now we come out of Mass, and go home. Then we come down here later for our dinner.

Martina: Yes, we have our dinner here now every Sunday. We bring the dessert. So if it's a dessert that needs to be made fresh, we'll make it when we get home after Mass. Otherwise we make it the day before.

Where do you get your recipes?

Martina: We get our recipes from cookbooks, and we have a lot of cookbooks, but almost all of the recipes have our own added twist.

Colette: We never expected the idea for this book to go further than having a few copies made for the Jesuits in different locations, but Simon saw it had the potential to be published. Then, Dries (Dries van den Akker SJ) came on board, and he and Joe (Joseph Munitiz SJ) put a huge amount of work into gathering saints to go with every dish in the book.

Conclusion

While at Colette and Martina's house, Simon Bishop SJ (below) and I were treated to tea and buns. The use of rosewater in their cake mixture was delicious. They explained that when you add rosewater to cake mixture, the mixture will never overflow the container, be that a cake container or a simple paper bun case. In their kitchen there were three cakes sitting waiting to be decorated, and a tin of buns, half of them beautifully decorated with a Christmas theme. Martina had decorated a sweet tin with Christmas paper and cut-outs of a Christmas tree and other festive images.

Simon Bishop SJ chatting with Colette and Martina's at their home.

SAINT BRIGID OF KILDARE   SAINT CONRAD   SAINT EVE

CHOOSING THE SAINTS

DRIES VAN DEN AKKER SJ

In my former life I taught religion at Stanislas College, a Jesuit college in Delft, in the Netherlands. I liked to open my lessons by telling stories, especially saints' stories, and particularly the stories of the saints after whom my pupils were named. I liked to tell their stories, for they reflect the faithful life of the storyteller. I found spiritual food in all the stories.

When Martina and Colette heard this, they asked me to find a suitable saint for every recipe in their cookbook. That was a lovely challenge: to show that the treasure of our faith can be enjoyed with playfulness. The art was to find a saint for the recipes. Sometimes the connection with a saint was easy: any fish could be connected with Saint Peter; salmon could go with Saint Mungo, because a salmon plays an important role in his story. A recipe with sunflower oil had to be connected with Saint Francis, for sunflowers follow the sun during the day, reminding us of how Christians have to follow Jesus. But which saint is associated with ginger? Well, we know that some saints had ginger hair! And what to do with tomato soup? There wasn't any saint who could be associated with tomatoes. Fortunately, I knew a statue of the Madonna in a Dutch market-gardening district, which depicts Mary giving a tomato to the little Jesus!

Of course I wanted some Jesuit saints in the cookbook but the connection between Jesuit saints and recipes is extremely tenuous. With what recipe could I connect Father Ignatius? In his case the word 'sponge' gave the clue … The sizzling sausages provided a link to the very first martyr of the Jesuit order, Antonio Criminali; he is not a saint, but a servant of God. What has he to do with 'sizzling sausages'? He was born in the Italian city of Sissa …

In the Jesuit Constitutions Saint Ignatius writes [251]: 'While the meal is being eaten, food should be given also to the soul … .' May this book be a contribution to ours.

The kitchen at Manresa.

BLESSING OF THE KITCHEN

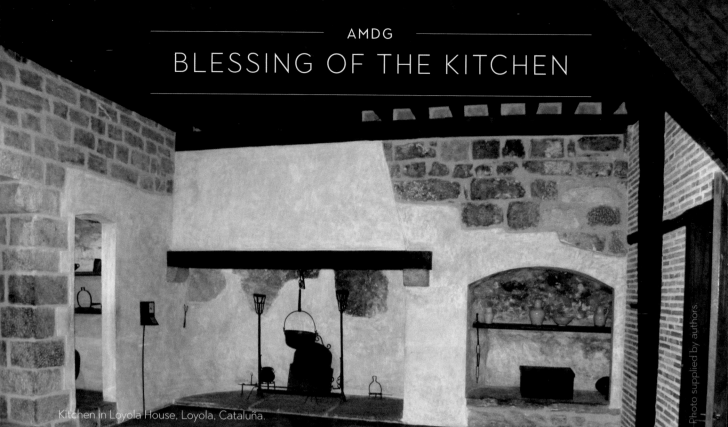

Kitchen in Loyola House, Loyola, Cataluña.

Photo supplied by authors.

Be present, Spirit of God, within us,
your dwelling place and home,
that this house may be one where
all darkness is penetrated by your light;
all troubles calmed by your peace;
all evil redeemed by your love;
all pain transformed by your suffering
and all dying glorified by your risen life.

Blessed are you, plentiful God,
for you supply our every need
according to your great riches.

May this kitchen always be filled
with the produce of the earth,
and may the preparations here
be filled with pleasure and love.
Bless the hands that work in this place,
and fill us with gratitude for your provision.

May this kitchen be so filled with peace
that all who eat food prepared here receive happiness.
May this kitchen be so filled with good will
that working here is a joy.

Bless this kitchen.
Bless all who work here.
Bless the food that is prepared here.
May this kitchen and the work done here
be a blessing to all who live.

May the eye of God be dwelling with you;
The foot of Christ in guidance with you;
The shower of the Spirit pouring on you;
And be the sacred Three
To save, to shield, to surround
the hearth, the house, the household,
this day, this night
and every day and night.

GRACE BEFORE & AFTER MEALS

GRACE BEFORE MEALS

Oh, God!
May the God who is One and Three
Bless our food
and you and me:
Father, Son and Holy Spirit
The One and the Three

GRACE AFTER MEALS

Praise to God,
peace to the living
and rest to those who have died

Our Father...

May Christ Jesus give us
holy peace,
blessing
and after death eternal life.
Amen!

Blessed the womb of the Virgin Mary,
which bore the Son of the eternal Father.
Amen!

TOMATO & QUINOA SOUP

Serves 10

3 x 400g tins chopped tomatoes
3 carrots, diced
3 celery sticks, diced
2 onions, diced
3 garlic cloves, crushed
2tsp dried oregano
3tsp reduced-salt vegetable stock powder
3tbsp thick balsamic vinegar
6tbsp shredded fresh basil
100g quinoa
2tbsp shredded fresh mint
2tbsp shredded fresh flatleaf parsley
10 thin slices granary bread, toasted, to serve

1. Put a large pan over a medium-high heat, then add the tomatoes, carrots, celery, onion, garlic and oregano. Mix the stock with 1ltr boiling water in a jug, then add to the pan along with the vinegar and half the basil. Bring to the boil, then reduce the heat and simmer for 20-25 min until the soup thickens.

2. Meanwhile, cook the quinoa in a medium pan according to the pack instructions. Drain.

    Take the soup off the heat and purée with a stick blender (or leave to cool slightly and whiz in a food processor). Stir the quinoa into the soup with most of the remaining basil, the mint and parsley.

    Garnish with the remaining basil and a grind of pepper, then serve with the toast.

CHEESE TOPPED MUSHROOMS WITH SMASHED SQUASH

Serves 10

A great lunch or lighter evening meal.

2kg butternut squash
4tbls olive oil
500g ricotta
5tsp fresh thyme
2 eggs
1tbls Dijon mustard
30g parmesan-style cheese, finely grated
20 large Portobello mushrooms, caps left whole, stems removed and finely chopped
2 tbls chopped fresh rosemary
5tsp pine nuts
1 small red chilli, thinly sliced
700g tenderstem broccoli, trimmed
A few sprigs of fresh basil to garnish

1. Heat the oven to 200oC /fan 180oC/gas 6. Line 2 large baking trays with baking paper. Put the squash on 1 tray and drizzle with half the olive oil. Bake for 30 mins or until golden and tender.

2. Meanwhile, in a bowl combine the ricotta mixture, thyme, egg, mustard and half the grated cheese, then fold in the mushroom stems and season with black pepper.

3. Fill the mushroom caps with the ricotta mixture. Transfer to the second prepared tray and scatter over the remaining grated cheese. Bake for the last 20-25 min of the squash cooking time.

4. A few mins before the squash and mushrooms are cooked, het the remaining oil in a non-stick frying pan over a medium-high heat. Fry the rosemary, pine nuts and chilli, stirring, until golden. Steam the tenderstem broccoli until tender, then drain.

5. Transfer the roasted squash to a bowl and mash roughly with a fork. Season with pepper and scatter with the rosemary mixture.

6. Serve the mushrooms with squash and broccoli, garnish with basil.

THE HOLY VIRGIN

**MARY, THE MOTHER OF GOD
FEAST DAY: 1 JANUARY**

Devotion to Mary has an important place for Jesuits. In the 'Meditation on the Two Standards' in his *Spiritual Exercises* St Ignatius explains how to pray to Our Lady, making a colloquy and asking for her help:

> I beg her to obtain for me grace from her Son and Lord that I may be received under His standard; first, in the highest spiritual poverty; and also, if His Divine Majesty requires this and should be pleased to choose and receive me for it, in actual poverty; second, in suffering insults and reproaches, so as to imitate Him more closely, provided only that I can suffer these without sin on the part of any other person and without displeasure to His Divine Majesty. Then I will say a Hail Mary. (Exx. 147)

The first church that the Jesuits took over in Rome was dedicated to Our Lady of the Way, a title that fitted perfectly with what the Jesuits called from the beginning 'our way of proceeding'. Unlike the form of religious life that had existed up to the time of St Ignatius — when members of religious orders met seven times a day for the singing of the Office — Jesuits were to be free to go out to the people in order to bring them a sense of God; they said their Office when they could, in private.

However, what does Our Lady have to do with tomatoes? In the parish church of Bergschenhoek, near Rotterdam in the Netherlands, there is a side altar dedicated to the Holy Virgin with representations of some stories about the young Jesus. Because the main industry of the village of Bergschenhoek is market gardening, these stories are in a setting where vegetables and fruit are important, and so the Holy Virgin gives the child Jesus not an apple, but a tomato.

CREAMY TOMATO SOUP

1. Melt the butter in a large saucepan. Add the onion and cook for 5 minutes until softened.
2. Stir in the tomatoes, carrots, stock, parsley and thyme. Bring to the boil. Reduce the heat to low, cover the pan, and simmer for 15–20 minutes until the vegetables are tender.
3. Purée the soup until it is smooth, then return to the pan.
4. Stir in the cream, if using, and reheat gently. Season the soup to taste with salt and pepper. Ladle into warmed soup bowls and serve piping hot, garnished with thyme leaves.

25g/1oz butter or margarine
1 large onion, chopped
900g/2lb tomatoes, peeled and quartered
2 carrots, chopped
450ml/16fl oz vegetable stock
2 tbsp chopped fresh parsley
½ tsp fresh thyme leaves, plus extra to garnish
5 tbsp single cream (optional)
salt and freshly ground black pepper

Serves 4
Preparation: 15–20 minutes
Cooking: 35–40 minutes

SAINT
SAINT AETHELBERT

SAINT AETHELBERT (+606)
FEAST DAY: 24 FEBRUARY

Saint Aethelbert is chosen for a reason that can only be described as fortuitous: his name is the Old English equivalent of 'Albert' and the street in which this book of recipes has been created is Albert Road, the home of the novices in the UK.

However, mushrooms, one of the main ingredients in the recipe, are known to grow best in times of peace and balanced government, and surely the reign of good King Aethelbert is a prime example of this! Even before his conversion, he was famed as a wise and peaceful ruler. It was he who, thanks to his Christian wife, Queen Bertha, welcomed Saint Augustine of Canterbury, sent by Gregory the Great to convert the angelic 'Angli'. The pope's advice had been, 'Destroy their idols, but not their sanctuaries! Sprinkle them with holy water and the people, seeing the holy places still standing, will come with joyful hearts.' When the king embraced the Christian faith, he did not force his people to follow his example. Saint Paul's Cathedral was built under his rule, and many churches bear the name of 'Albert'.

BLACK PUDDING WITH FIELD MUSHROOMS, POACHED EGG & APPLE SLICES

1. Preheat the grill. To prepare the mushrooms, remove the stalks and carefully peel the caps. Put the mushrooms on a baking sheet, brush with melted butter and cook under a medium grill for 10 minutes, turning once.
2. Meanwhile, melt the lard in a frying pan, add the black pudding slices and fry for 3 minutes on each side.
3. Melt the butter in a separate small frying pan, add the apple slices and gently cook until just soft and beginning to turn a golden brown.
4. Bring a saucepan of water to a gentle simmer then add the vinegar. Carefully crack the eggs into the water and poach gently for about 3 minutes until the whites are just set (you may find it easier to poach just two eggs at a time).
5. To serve, place the mushrooms, cup side uppermost, on four warmed serving plates and top each with a slice of black pudding. Place a poached egg on top. Arrange the apple slices at the side. Season generously with pepper, garnish with parsley sprigs and serve immediately.

4 field mushrooms or open cup mushrooms
15g/½oz melted butter
25g/1oz lard or bacon fat
4 slices black pudding
15g/½oz butter
2 eating apples, peeled, cored and sliced
1 tbsp malt vinegar
4 eggs
freshly ground black pepper
fresh parsley sprigs, to garnish

Serves 4
Preparation: 5 minutes
Cooking: 15 minutes

SAINT WILGEFORTIS

SAINT WILGEFORTIS (+139)
(SAINT CUCUMBER)
FEAST DAY: 20 JULY

Wilgefortis was the daughter of the King of Portugal. She became a Christian in secret and in her prayers promised to remain a virgin out of ardent love for Christ. However, the King of Sicily unexpectedly asked her father for her hand in marriage. When she refused, saying that she had no intention of marrying, her father was furious. He had her flogged and then imprisoned her in a dark dungeon to make her change her mind.

Wilgefortis turned to prayer and implored God to make her so unattractive that no one, and least of all the King of Sicily, would want to marry her. She began to sprout a huge beard. When her father saw what had happened and learned that it was because of her devotion to Christ, he decided that she would have to suffer like Christ, and he had her crucified.

Connected with this is a story about the *Volto Santo*, a crucifix that is venerated in the Italian city of Lucca. Christ is represented wearing what looks like a long female dress, and pilgrims from outside Italy seem to have misinterpreted this as the image of a crucified woman with a beard: she was adopted as a patron saint against all kinds of distress and is known in Dutch-speaking countries as Saint Ontkommer, because in Dutch, the word ontkommer means 'anti-distress' (*kommer* = 'distress').

From *ontkommer*, or 'un-cumber', it was only a short step to 'cu-cumber', and hence the connection between Saint Cucumber (Saint Wilgefortis) and 'cucumber mousse'.

CUCUMBER MOUSSE

1. Peel the cucumber, leaving a little of the green skin, then halve lengthways and remove the seeds. Finely chop the flesh and set aside to drain.
2. Blend the cheese until soft, then stir in the mayonnaise. Add the water to a small bowl, then sprinkle the gelatine into it. Place the bowl over a saucepan of hot water and stir until the gelatine is dissolved. Add the salt and sugar, stir and leave to cool.
3. Whip the cream until it holds soft peaks. Stir the cooled gelatine mixture into the mayonnaise and cheese mixture, add the chopped cucumber and fold in the cream. Mix thoroughly.
4. Pour the mixture into a dampened 1 litre/1¾ pint ring mould. Chill until firm. Turn out onto a plate, garnish with cucumber slices and serve.

1 large cucumber
225g/8oz full-fat soft cheese
150ml/5fl oz lemon mayonnaise
150ml/5fl oz water
1 sachet gelatine
½ tsp salt
2 tsp caster sugar
150ml/5fl oz double cream
cucumber slices, to garnish

Serves 6
Preparation: 20 minutes
Chilling: 2–3 hours

SAINT DAVID THE KING

SAINT DAVID (+960 BC)
FEAST DAY: 29 DECEMBER

A Bible passage provides a hook for this recipe: it describes how King David brought the Ark to Jerusalem: 'And David danced whirling round before Yahweh with all his might, wearing a linen loincloth' (although our illustration shows him in kingly attire playing his harp!). To close the celebrations the text mentions that David 'then distributed to each a loaf of bread, a portion of dates and a raisin cake. Then the people all went back to their homes' (2 Samuel 6:12–19). Of course, the possibility that David was dancing a salsa makes him even more appropriate as a patron for this recipe.

MANGO, MELON, RAISIN & FRESH TOMATO SALSA

Tip:
This salsa is very good served with cold meat

1. Score a cross in the base of each tomato. Place the tomatoes in a bowl of boiling water for 10 seconds, then plunge into cold water and peel the skin away from the cross. Scoop out the seeds and discard. Finely chop the flesh.
2. Peel, stone and finely dice the mango. Peel, deseed and finely dice the melon.
3. Mix the mango and melon with the tomatoes, raisins and cucumber.
4. Mix together the lemon rind, vinegar and oil and add to the salsa. Season well and scatter with the spring onion to serve.

2 tomatoes

1 very ripe mango

1 very ripe melon

50g/1¾oz raisins

1 cucumber, cut into small
   pieces

1 tsp finely grated lemon rind

2 tbsp red wine vinegar

1 tbsp olive oil

1 spring onion, shredded

Serves 4
Preparation: 20 minutes

SAINT FRANCIS OF ASSISI

SAINT FRANCIS OF ASSISI (+1226)
FEAST DAY: 4 OCTOBER

Saint Francis chose the sunflower as the symbol of his spirituality, because the sunflower follows 'Brother Sun' from east to west, keeping its face always turned towards the sun. So did Francis with Christ. His famous 'Canticle of the Sun' has the words:

> Be praised, my Lord, through all your creatures,
> especially through my lord Brother Sun,
> who brings the day; and you give light through him.
> And he is beautiful and radiant in all his splendour!
> Of you, Most High, he bears the likeness.

One of the ingredients of this soup is sunflower oil, which justifies the invocation of this great saint.

SWEET POTATO & PARSNIP SOUP

1. Heat the oil in a large saucepan and add the leek, celery, sweet potatoes and parsnips. Cook gently for about 5 minutes, stirring to prevent them browning or sticking to the pan.

2. Stir in the chicken stock and bring to the boil, then cover and simmer gently for about 25 minutes, or until the vegetables are tender, stirring occasionally. Season to taste with salt and pepper. Remove the pan from the heat and leave the soup to cool slightly.

3. Purée the soup in a blender or food processor until smooth, then return the soup to the pan and reheat gently. Ladle into warmed soup bowls and garnish with chopped parsley, roasted vegetable strips and lemon slices, if using, and serve immediately.

1 tbsp sunflower oil
1 large leek, sliced
2 celery sticks, chopped
450g/1lb sweet potatoes, diced
225g/8oz parsnips, diced
850ml/1½ pints chicken stock
salt and freshly ground white
  pepper

Garnish
1 tbsp chopped fresh parsley
roasted strips of sweet
  potatoes and parsnips
  (optional)
Lemon slices

Serves 6
Preparation: 20 minutes
Cooking 40–50 minutes, plus
  cooling

SAINT JACOB

SAINT JACOB

FEAST DAY: 5 FEBRUARY/6 OCTOBER

One of the best-known Old Testament stories recounts how Jacob took over the birthright of his older brother Esau (Genesis 25:29–34).

Once, when Jacob was cooking a stew, Esau returned from the countryside exhausted. Esau said to Jacob, 'Give me a mouthful of that red stuff there; I am exhausted.'

Jacob said, 'First, give me your birthright in exchange.'

Esau said, 'Here I am, at death's door; what use is a birthright to me?'

Then Jacob said, 'First give me your oath'; he gave him his oath and sold his birthright to Jacob.

Then Jacob gave him some bread and lentil stew; he ate, drank, got up and went away.

Jacob's soup is said to have been a lentil soup, but it was the same colour as this carrot and coriander soup (between orange and red), and our hope is that it will be equally irresistible.

The feast of the holy patriarch Jacob was celebrated in the past either on 6 October, together with Abraham and Isaac, or on 5 February, together with Abraham and Sarah, Lot and Melchisedek, Isaac and Rachel, and the twelve sons of Jacob.

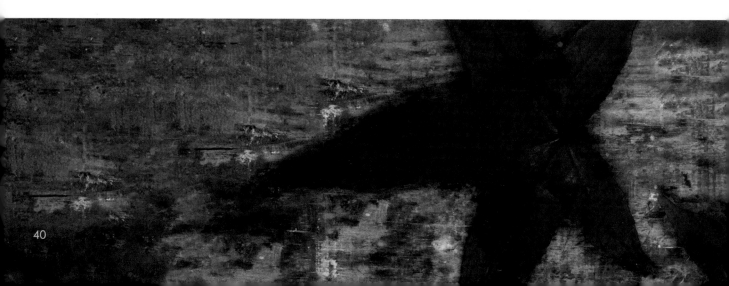

CARROT & CORIANDER SOUP

1. Melt the butter in a large saucepan. Add the leeks and carrots and stir well. Cover and cook for 10 minutes, until the vegetables are beginning to soften.
2. Stir in the ground coriander and cook for about 1 minute. Pour in the stock and season to taste with salt and pepper. Bring to the boil, cover and simmer for about 20 minutes, until the leeks and carrots are tender.
3. Leave to cool slightly, then purée the soup in a blender until smooth. Return the soup to the pan and add 2 tablespoons of the yogurt, then taste the soup and adjust the seasoning. Reheat gently, but do not boil.
4. Ladle the soup into warmed bowls and put a spoonful of the remaining yogurt in the centre of each. Garnish with coriander and serve immediately.

55g/2oz butter
3 leeks, sliced
450g/1lb carrots, sliced
1 tbsp ground coriander
1.2 litres/2 pints chicken stock
150ml/5fl oz Greek-style yogurt
salt and freshly ground black
   pepper
fresh coriander sprigs, to
   garnish

Serves 4
Preparation: 10 minutes
Cooking: 40–45 minutes, plus
   cooling

SAINT ALEXANDER

SAINT ALEXANDER (+1229)
FEAST DAY: 3 MAY

Alexander was a Scottish prince from a very pious family. His two older brothers had chosen to live as monks and he had a sister, Saint Mechtild, who became a nun. She urged Alexander, the youngest in the family, to give up material things for the sake of the heavenly. Young Alexander loved the beauty of natural things and asked his sister what he should do. She took him to a farm where he learned to milk the cows and to make butter and cheese. Eventually Mechtild and Alexander crossed to France where he joined the Cistercian monastery of Foigny, near Laon in northern France. There, Alexander lived as a simple lay brother, taking care of the cattle — and helping to produce cheese!

CHEESE SOUFFLÉ

1. Preheat the oven to 190°C/375°F/Gas 6. Grease an 850 ml/1½ pint soufflé dish or a pie dish.
2. Place the milk, butter and flour in a saucepan over a medium heat and whisk until blended and thickened. Reduce the heat to low and cook for a further 3 minutes, stirring occasionally. Stir in the cayenne pepper, mustard and nutmeg and season to taste with salt and pepper.
3. Leave the sauce to cool a little before stirring in the Cheddar cheese. Beat the egg yolks thoroughly, then stir them into the mixture.
4. Whisk the egg whites until stiff peaks hold. Beat a couple of spoonfuls into the sauce, then fold in the remainder gently and carefully so you don't lose all the precious air. Transfer the mixture to the prepared dish, place on a baking sheet in the centre of the preheated oven and bake for 30–35 minutes.
5. The soufflé is cooked when a skewer inserted into the centre comes out fairly clean. Be careful not to overcook: it should be soft, not dry, in the centre. Serve immediately with a little dish of Parmesan cheese and a salad.

150ml/5fl oz milk

25g/1oz butter, plus extra for greasing

25g/1oz plain flour

pinch of cayenne pepper

¼ tsp dry mustard powder

a little freshly grated nutmeg

85g/3oz hard cheese, such as Cheddar, grated

3 large eggs, separated

salt and freshly ground black pepper

freshly grated Parmesan cheese and a salad, to serve

Serves 3–4
Preparation: 10–15 mins
Cooking: 30–35 mins

FISH

SAINT CORENTIN

SAINT CORENTIN OF QUIMPER (+490)
FEAST DAY: 12 DECEMBER

Saint Corentin helped found the Church in Brittany, France. Among the stories about him there is one about his keeping a fish pond, in which his pet fish swam. This kindly fish was happy for his master to cut off a slice of him each day for his meal – the creature suffered no harm in the process. When the king heard of this marvel, he wanted to see it for himself, so he paid a visit to Bishop Corentin with all his court. When the royal cook asked what food to prepare, Corentin presented him with one slice of fish. The cook roared with laughter and said, 'What am I supposed to do with this morsel for all these people?' 'Just cook it and see what happens,' replied the bishop. As the cooking progressed the piece of fish multiplied and finally all present had more than enough to eat – though the royal cook was very embarrassed. The moral of the story is very simple: in the case of every saint, Christ is present and can work marvels.

SEA BASS WITH CITRUS FRUIT

1. Preheat the oven to 190°C/375°F/Gas 5. Using a vegetable peeler, remove the rind from the grapefruit, orange and lemon. Cut the rind into thin julienne strips, cover and set aside. Peel the white pith from the fruits and, working over a bowl to catch the juices, cut out the segments from the grapefruit and orange and set aside for the garnish. Reserve the juices. Cut the lemon into thick slices.
2. Wipe the fish dry inside and out and season the cavity with a little salt and pepper. Make three diagonal slashes on each side. Reserve a few basil and dill sprigs for the garnish and fill the cavity with the remaining basil and dill, the lemon slices and half the citrus rind.
3. Lightly dust the fish with flour. In a roasting tin or flameproof casserole large enough to hold the fish, heat 2 tablespoons of the oil over a medium-high heat and cook the fish for about 1 minute until the skin just crisps and browns on one side. Add the shallots.
4. Bake in the preheated oven for about 15 minutes, then carefully turn the fish over and stir the shallots. Drizzle the fish with the remaining oil and bake for a further 10–15 minutes until the flesh is opaque throughout.
5. Carefully transfer the fish to a warmed serving dish and remove and discard the cavity stuffing. Pour off any excess oil and add the wine and 2–3 tablespoons of the reserved fruit juices to the pan. Bring to the boil over a high heat, stirring. Stir in the remaining citrus rind and boil for 2–3 minutes, then whisk in the butter. Spoon the shallots and sauce around the fish and garnish with the reserved herbs and grapefruit and orange segments.

1 small grapefruit

1 orange

1 lemon

1 sea bass, about 1.3kg/3lb, cleaned and scaled

6 fresh basil sprigs

6 fresh dill sprigs

plain flour, for dusting

3 tbsp olive oil

4–6 shallots, halved

4 tbsp dry white wine

15g/½oz butter

salt and freshly ground black pepper

Serves 6
Preparation: 20 minutes
Cooking: 35–40 minutes

SAINT
SAINT FREDERICK

SAINT FREDERICK
BISHOP OF UTRECHT (+838)
FEAST DAY: 18 JULY

According to one legend, Frederick was invited by King Louis the Pious of France to share a meal. The king then invited the saintly bishop to preach the Gospel throughout his realm and to counter all abuses. To the king's surprise, Frederick pointed to the salmon on the table and asked, 'When you eat a fish, your Majesty, do you start with the head or with the tail?' 'Obviously with the head, as that is where there is more flesh,' replied the king. 'Quite,' said the bishop. 'So let me start immediately with you, the head: your marriage with Lady Judith is illegal according to the Church because you are too closely related.'

Lady Judith was so angry that she hired two assassins who murdered the outspoken bishop in his cathedral. The image here shows him with a k

SALMON STEAKS WITH HERB BUTTER SAUCE

1. Bring a saucepan of lightly salted water to the boil. Add the carrots, bring back to the boil and cook for 1 minute; drain and set aside.
2. Heat the oil with 25g/1oz of the butter in a frying pan until the butter has melted. Sprinkle the salmon steaks with a little salt and pepper to taste, add to the pan and fry for 5–7 minutes on each side. Transfer to a warmed serving dish and keep warm.
3. Cut the cucumber in half lengthways, then remove the seeds and cut into 1 cm/½ inch slices. Add to the pan with the carrots and wine, cover and cook for 4–5 minutes. Remove the carrots and cucumber with a slotted spoon and arrange around the fish; keep warm. Boil the liquor in the pan until it has reduced to 2 tablespoons.
4. Beat together the dill, chives and the remaining butter in a bowl. Beat in the reduced liquor until a smooth, thick sauce forms. Spoon over the salmon, garnish with dill and grapefruit and orange segments and serve immediately.

250g/9oz carrots, cut into fine julienne strips
1 tbsp olive oil
85g/3oz unsalted butter
6 x 175g/6oz salmon steaks
350g/12oz cucumber, peeled
150ml/5fl oz dry white wine
1 tbsp snipped fresh chives
2 tsps chopped dill
salt and freshly ground black pepper
fresh dill sprigs and grapefruit and orange segments, to garnish

Serves 6
Preparation: 20 minutes
Cooking: 25–30 minutes

SAINT MUNGO

SAINT MUNGO (+612)
FEAST DAY: 13 JANUARY

Saint Mungo, also known as Kentigern, is venerated as the founder of the city of Glasgow in Scotland. Thanks to the story about Saint Mungo and the salmon, this fish figures in the city's coat-of-arms.

According to legend, the King of Strathclyde suspected his wife of infidelity; he arranged for her wedding ring to be stolen and then had it thrown into the River Clyde. He upbraided the queen because she no longer wore her wedding ring and threatened her with death if she did not find it.

The queen turned for help to Saint Mungo/Kentigern, who told one of his monks to fish in the river. Sure enough, a salmon was caught, and when it was cut open, it was found to contain the ring, so the queen was able to clear her name.

SALMON WITH CUCUMBER SAUCE

1. Preheat the oven to 220°C/425°F/Gas 7. Season the salmon and brush inside and out with melted butter. Place the parsley and lemon in the cavity.
2. Wrap the salmon in foil, folding the edges together securely, then bake in the preheated oven for 15 minutes. Remove the fish from the oven and leave to rest in the foil for 1 hour, then remove the skin from the salmon.
3. Meanwhile, to make the sauce, halve the cucumber lengthways, remove the seeds and dice the flesh.
4. Place the cucumber in a colander, toss lightly with salt, leave to drain for about 30 minutes, then rinse well and pat dry.
5. Heat the butter in a small saucepan, add the cucumber and cook for about 2 minutes until translucent but not soft. Add the wine to the pan and boil briskly until it has evaporated.
6. Stir the dill and sour cream into the cucumber mixture. Season to taste and serve immediately with the salmon.

1.8kg/4lb whole salmon, cleaned and scaled
melted butter, for brushing
3 fresh parsley sprigs
½ lemon, halved
salt and freshly ground black pepper

Sauce
1 large cucumber, peeled
25g/1oz butter
115ml/4fl oz dry white wine
3 tbsp finely chopped fresh dill
4 tbsp sour cream
salt

Serves 6–8
Preparation: 25–30 minutes, plus 1 hour's cooling
Cooking: 20 minutes

SAINT PETER

SAINT PETER, PATRON OF
FISHERMEN (+1ST CENTURY)
FEAST DAY: 29 JUNE
(TOGETHER WITH SAINT PAUL)

As a fisherman, Saint Peter was well acquainted with fish. He was invited by Jesus 'to fish people' instead (Mark 1:17). He became the leader of the twelve apostles, but remained a humble man. The proof lies in the fact that the Gospel of Saint Mark (said to be linked to the preaching of Peter) contains the account of Peter denying Jesus (Mark 14:66–71).

Saint Thérèse of Lisieux pondered why Peter had to endure such a humiliation. Her answer was that, because he was destined to be the leader of the Church, that is to say the leader of those who know that they are sinners and need forgiveness, it made sense that he should learn by experience what it means to be forgiven!

In the twentieth century when scholars excavated under the high altar of St Peter's Basilica in Rome they discovered the bones of a man who had come from the east in the first century and was accustomed to standing in water; the bones showed traces of arthrosis. It is surely a comforting thought that the Church was founded on the bones of a man suffering from arthrosis!

HALIBUT WITH FENNEL & ORANGE

1. Preheat the oven to 180°C/350°F/Gas 4. Grease a shallow baking dish.
2. Bring a small saucepan of water to the boil, add the fennel, bring back to the boil and boil for 4–6 minutes until just tender.
3. Meanwhile, put the orange juice and rind into a saucepan with the wine and cook until reduced by half.
4. Drain the fennel well, then spread in the baking dish and season to taste with salt and pepper. Arrange the halibut on the fennel, season to taste with salt and pepper, dot with butter and pour over the orange and wine reduction.
5. Cover with foil and bake in the preheated oven for 15–20 minutes, or until the flesh flakes.
6. Serve immediately, garnished with fennel fronds and orange wedges.

1 fennel bulb, thinly sliced

juice and grated rind of 1 orange

150ml/5fl oz dry white wine

4 halibut steaks, about 200g/7oz each

55g/2oz butter, plus extra for greasing

salt and freshly ground black pepper

fennel fronds and orange wedges, to garnish

Serves 4
Preparation: 15 mins
Cooking: 15–20 mins

Photograph: Zoryanchik / Shutterstock

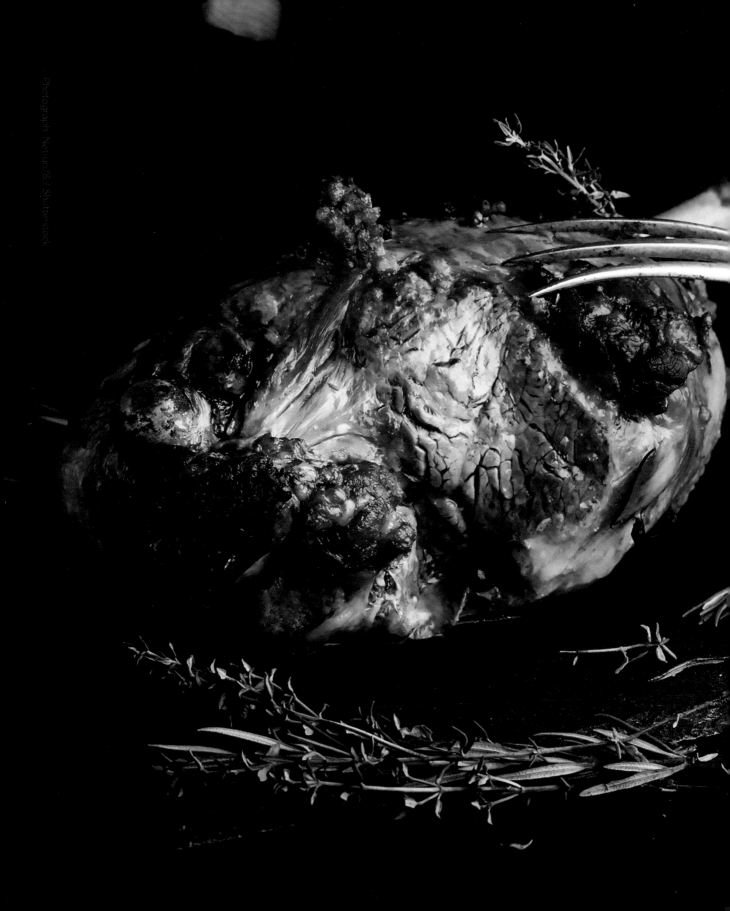

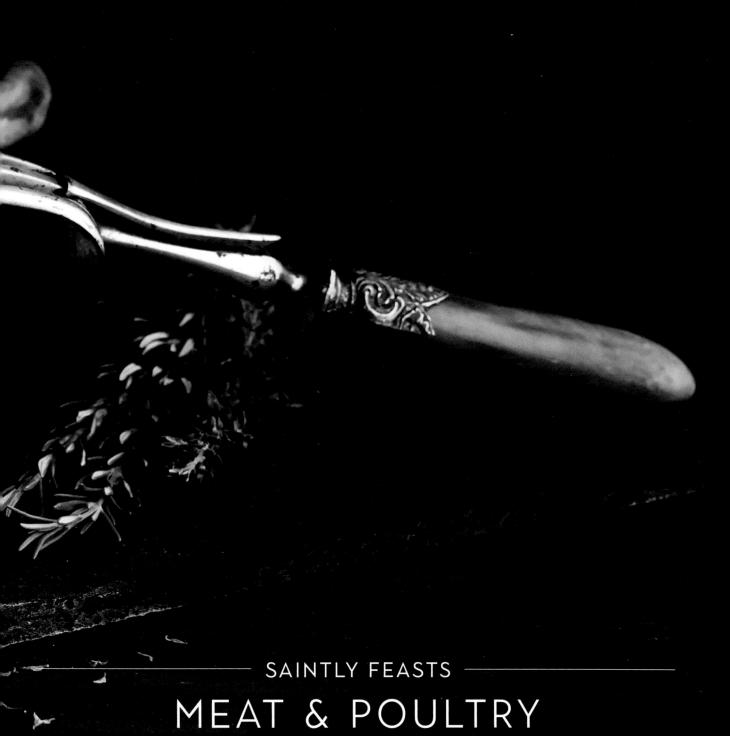

SAINTLY FEASTS

MEAT & POULTRY

SAINT AGNES

SAINT AGNES (+304)
FEAST DAY: 21 JANUARY

Saint Agnes was about thirteen years old when she was martyred during the persecution under the emperor Diocletian.

She is always represented with a lamb, because her name sounds like the Latin word 'agnus', meaning 'lamb'. In fact, her name is derived from the Greek word 'hagnós', meaning 'holy'.

If you are ever in the 6th-century basilica of Sant' Apollinare Nuovo in Ravenna, Italy, you will see that one of the mosaics depicts a procession of virgin martyrs. They are offering their martyr crowns to the little Jesus who is resting on the lap of his mother, Mary, the Queen of Heaven. One of these virgins is Saint Agnes with her lamb.

MARINATED LAMB CHOPS
AND PORT REDUCTION

1. Place the lamb chops in a shallow, non-metallic dish.
2. Combine the orange juice and zest, garlic, rosemary and salt and pepper to taste then pour the mixture over the chops.
3. Turn the chops to coat in the marinade. Cover and leave to marinate for at least 1 hour or overnight.
4. Preheat a griddle pan over a medium heat. Remove the chops from the marinade, reserving the marinade, and pat dry on kitchen paper.
5. Place the chops in the preheated pan and cook for 4–5 minutes on each side.
6. Meanwhile, pour the marinade into a small saucepan and stir in the port. Bring to the boil and continue to boil rapidly until reduced by half.
7. Stir in the cooking juices from the griddle pan, then cook over a low heat for 5 minutes.
8. Spoon the juices around the chops and serve with mint sauce and redcurrant jelly, if liked.

4–8 lamb chops or cutlets

juice and grated zest of 1 orange

1 garlic clove, chopped

1 tbsp chopped fresh rosemary

8 tbsp port

4 tbsp redcurrant jelly, plus extra to serve (optional)

2 tbsp lemon juice

salt and freshly ground black pepper

mint sauce, to serve (optional)

Serves 4

Preparation: 5–10 minutes, plus 1 hour's marinating

Cooking: 10–12 minutes

Photograph: Foxys Forest Manufacture / Shutterstock

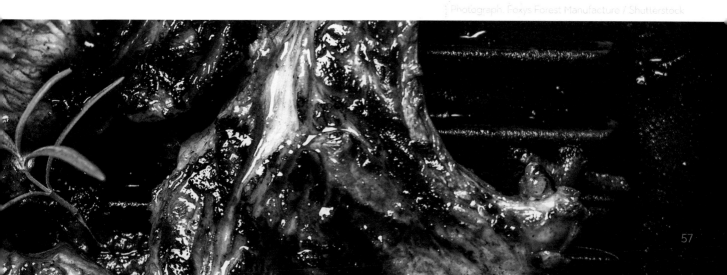

SAINT ANTHONY THE ABBOT

SAINT ANTHONY, ABBOT (+356)
FEAST DAY: 17 JANUARY

Saint Anthony, also called the Great, is not to be confused with Saint Anthony of Padua (helpful finder of lost things). Saint Anthony the Abbot was one of the first Christian hermits and his life is well known thanks to the book about him written by his bishop, Saint Athanasius of Alexandria.

When Anthony heard of the persecution of Christians (about the year 310) he went to Alexandria hoping to die as a martyr. However, as the authorities were not interested in him, he retired to live as a solitary in the desert, fasting and practising much physical mortification. But his mind continued to plague him with all sorts of temptations, vividly represented by many painters.

In one such picture he is shown simply with a fire, to represent the force of passion, and with a pig as a symbol of the unclean thoughts that troubled him. Thus Anthony is considered the patron saint of pigs.

No doubt one of the temptations that came to him in his fasting was to indulge in eating, and it is to be hoped that the present recipe will be used with moderation.

ROAST PORK

1. Unwrap the joint and place uncovered on a plate until required. This allows the skin to dry and improves the crackling. If you are cooking immediately, dab the joint dry with kitchen paper.
2. Preheat the oven to 220°C/425°F/Gas 7. Weigh the joint and calculate the cooking time. Allow 25 minutes per 500g/1lb 2oz, plus 25 minutes.
3. Place the meat in a roasting tin, sprinkle the skin with a little salt and drizzle with a little rapeseed oil. Roast in the preheated oven for 1 hour, basting once or twice during cooking, then reduce the oven temperature to 180°C/350°F/Gas 4 for the remaining cooking time. The juices should run clear when the meat is pierced with a skewer and the crackling should be crispy.
4. Separate the crackling from the pork, then cover the meat with foil. Leave to rest for 15 minutes before carving.
5. To make the gravy, stir the flour into the roasting tin and cook for a few seconds over a low heat. Add the stock and cook, stirring until the gravy thickens.

boneless shoulder or leg pork joint, about 1.3–1.5kg/3–3lb 5oz
rapeseed oil, for drizzling
1 tbsp plain flour
300ml/10fl oz chicken or vegetable stock
salt

Serves 6–8
Preparation: 5 minutes
Cooking: 1 hour 25 minutes to 1 hour 40 minutes, plus 15 minutes' resting

SAINT COLETTE

SAINT COLETTE (+1477)
FEAST DAY: 6 MARCH

Saint Colette was the only child of two elderly parents. In honour of the saint they called her Nicolette, but this was soon shortened to Colette.

As an adult Colette decided to join a religious order and eventually founded a strict branch of the Order of Poor Clares, who became known as the Colettines. She died in Ghent in 1477.

In the image depicted here she is represented carrying a lamb, and thus her name is given to this recipe. However, this entry also serves as a tribute to Colette Scully, one of the two ladies responsible for this publication. With her friend and companion, Martina Maher, she has gathered and cooked all these recipes.

GRILLED LEG OF LAMB

1. Rub the lamb all over with oil, sprinkle with lemon juice, and scatter over the fresh herbs. Season with pepper to taste. Leave to stand for 1 hour before grilling.
2. Preheat the grill to high and lay the lamb on the rack, skin side up. Grill for about 15 minutes on each side, depending on how you like your lamb cooked. Leave to rest, loosely covered with a sheet of foil, in a warm place for at least 10–15 minutes.
3. Lay the lamb on a board to carve into neat 7 mm/¾ inch slices. Serve with a potato purée or a purée of root vegetables, a green salad and a fruit jelly.

1 small leg of lamb
4 tbsp rapeseed oil
juice of 1 lemon
a few fresh rosemary, marjoram and thyme sprigs
freshly ground black pepper

To serve
potato purée or purée of root vegetables
green salad
crab apple, mint or redcurrant jelly

Serves 6
Preparation: 5 minutes, plus 1 hour's standing
Cooking: 30–40 minutes, plus 10–15 minutes' resting

Photographs: DronG; Netrun78 / Shutterstock

SAINT EVE

SAINT EVE
FEAST DAY: 24 DECEMBER

In the past the Church had a feast day, 24 December, for Adam and Eve. Many an icon shows the Risen Lord giving them a helping hand when he descended into Hell.

Today's recipe, with its reference to the rib, may justify the choice of Eve as its patron. The account in Genesis of the creation of the woman is well known:

Then the Lord God said, 'It is not good that the man should be alone ... '. So the Lord God caused a deep sleep to fall upon the man and he slept; then he took one of his ribs and closed up its place with flesh. And the rib that the Lord God had taken from the man he made into a woman and brought her to the man. Then the man said: 'This at last is bone of my bones and flesh of my flesh; this one shall be called Woman, for out of Man this one was taken.' (Genesis 2:18–23)

ROAST PRIME RIB OF BEEF

1. Preheat the oven to 220°C/425°F/Gas 7. Sprinkle the beef fat with salt and pepper. Stand the joint on its end in a roasting tin just large enough for it on a bed of onion slices (the skin gives colour to the juices). Roast the beef in the centre of the oven for 15 minutes, then reduce the oven temperature to 180°C/350°F/Gas 4. Roast, basting from time to time. Roast for 15 minutes per 450g/1lb for rare; 20 minutes per 450g/1lb for medium; 25 minutes per 450g/1lb for well done.
2. Remove from the tin, loosely cover with foil and leave to rest in a warm place for 20 minutes. Discard the onion, squeezing any juices into the tin.
3. Meanwhile, make the gravy. Skim off 3 tablespoons of fat from the roasting tin and reserve. Pour all the remaining fat and juices into a bowl and chill in the refrigerator until the fat rises to the top. Measure the flour into the tin, add the reserved fat and whisk over a medium heat. Gradually add the port and stock, then the Worcestershire sauce. Skim the fat from the juices in the refrigerator and discard, then add the juices to the gravy, together with a little gravy browning. Check the seasoning.
4. To carve, slip a knife close to the bone to free the complete joint, then carve against the grain.

1 x 2-rib beef joint, either prime rib cut short, or wing rib cut short, about 2.25kg/5lb
1 large onion, unpeeled but thickly sliced
salt and freshly ground black pepper

Gravy
3 tbsp dripping from the roast
1 tbsp plain flour
75ml/2½fl oz port
500ml/18fl oz beef stock
dash of Worcestershire sauce
a little ready-made gravy browning

Serves 8
Preparation: 5 minutes
Cooking: 1 hour 25 minutes to
   2 hours, plus 20 minutes' resting

Photograph: Istetiana / Shutterstock

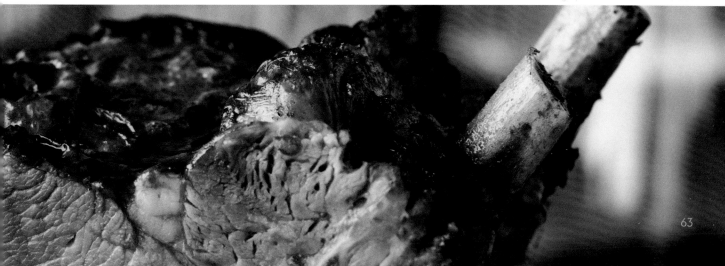

SAINT IDA

SAINT IDA (+1300)
FEAST DAY: 13 APRIL

Saint Ida was the daughter of a wine merchant in Leuven (Louvain) in Belgian Brabant. She decided to become a hermit and was so blessed by God that she was granted the stigmata.

However, one day when she went to pray in the church, there were so many cockerels and hens at the entrance that she could not enter. She spoke to the birds, telling them to refrain from their constant pecking for food; instead they were to come and listen to the Gospel, giving praise to their Creator. They all followed her into the church and stayed until after the reading of the Gospel, when she gave them permission to go out and resume their feeding.

In thanksgiving, let us remember the Creator and then enjoy chicken as in the recipe, with a glass of good wine in honour of Saint Ida.

In the Cistercian monastery in Steylaerts Kerniel, Belgium, there is a painting of Saint Ida in adoration before the altar with cross and flowers, praying: 'Dear Jesus, your love and nothing more!'

ROAST CHICKEN

1. Preheat the oven to 220°C/425°F/Gas 7. Make sure the chicken is clean, wiping it inside and out with kitchen paper, and place in a roasting tin. In a bowl, soften the butter with a fork, mix in the thyme and season well with salt and pepper. Butter the chicken all over with the herb butter, inside and out, and place the lemon pieces inside the body cavity. Pour the wine over the chicken.

2. Roast in the centre of the preheated oven for 20 minutes, then reduce the oven temperature to 190°C/375°F/Gas 5 and roast for a further 1¼ hours, basting frequently. Cover with foil if the skin begins to brown too much. If the tin dries out, add a little more wine or water. The chicken is cooked if the juices run clear when the thickest part of the leg is pierced with a sharp knife or skewer.

3. Remove from the oven, transfer to a warmed serving plate, cover loosely with foil and leave to rest for 20 minutes before carving.

4. Meanwhile, place the roasting tin on the top of the stove and bubble the pan juices gently over a low heat until they have reduced and are thick and glossy. Season to taste with salt and pepper.

5. Garnish the chicken with the thyme sprigs and serve immediately with the pan juices.

1 x 2.25kg/5lb free-range chicken

55g/2oz butter or a little rapeseed oil

2 tbsp chopped fresh lemon thyme

1 lemon, quartered

125ml/4fl oz white wine or water

salt and freshly ground black pepper

6 fresh thyme sprigs, to garnish

Serves 6
Preparation: 10 minutes
Cooking: 1 hour 35 minutes, plus 20 minutes' resting

SAINT MARGARET CLITHEROW

SAINT MARGARET CLITHEROW (+1586)
FEAST DAY: 25 OCTOBER

Saint Margaret was born in York to a Protestant family and married a butcher. She became a Roman Catholic, although this was forbidden, and insisted on bringing up her children in her own faith. Two of her sons became priests and one daughter entered a convent in Leuven (Louvain) in Belgium.

Her husband loved her dearly, as she had a radiant personality. He gave his silent consent while she helped to organise the celebration of mass, either in their house or wherever was safer. She not only took care of what was needed, but turned a room of the house into a classroom where children could be taught the Roman catechism, disregarding the danger.

Eventually the pursuivants (who hunted Catholics) burst into the house and questioned the children. They heard what they wanted and arrested Margaret. She was at once sentenced to death by being crushed under heavy stones. Her husband protested and offered all his wealth in return for his wife. 'She is the best wife in England as well as the best Catholic!' he cried out. One of the judges said to Margaret just before her execution, 'Remember that you die for treason!' 'No,' she replied, 'you know perfectly well that I am about to die for the love of Jesus.'

She died on Good Friday, 25 March 1586, and was canonised as one of the Forty Martyrs of England and Wales.

A good Yorkshire pudding can help to remind us of this heroic lady.

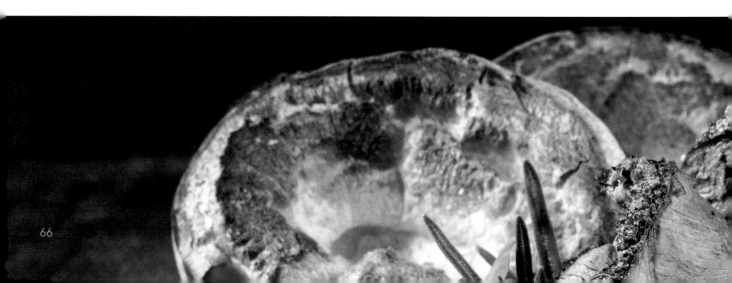

ROAST BEEF WITH YORKSHIRE PUDDINGS

1. Preheat the oven to 220°C/425°F/Gas 7. Heat the dripping in a roasting tin in the oven.
2. Place the meat on a rack, fat-side uppermost, then place the rack in the tin.
3. Baste the beef with the dripping, and roast, basting frequently, for 15 minutes per 450g/1lb plus 15 minutes for rare, 20 minutes per 450g/1lb plus 20 minutes for medium and 25–30 minutes per 450g/1lb plus 25 minutes for well done.
4. To make the Yorkshire puddings, stir the flour, salt and pepper together in a bowl and make a well in the centre. Pour the eggs into the well, then slowly pour in the milk, stirring until a smooth batter forms. Leave to stand for 30 minutes.
5. A few minutes before the meat is ready, spoon a little dripping into six patty tins and place in the oven until very hot. Remove the meat from the oven, then cover loosely with foil and keep warm.
6. Quickly pour the batter into the patty tins and bake for 15 minutes until well risen and brown.
7. Spoon off the fat from the roasting tin, Add the stock, stirring to dislodge the sediment, and boil for a few minutes. Check the seasoning and serve with the beef and Yorkshire puddings.

2–4 tbsp beef dripping or oil
1 x 1.8kg/4lb joint of beef
300ml/10fl oz vegetable or veal stock, wine or water
salt and freshly ground black pepper

Yorkshire Puddings
125g/4½oz plain flour
pinch of salt and pinch of freshly ground black pepper
2 eggs, beaten
125ml/4fl oz milk
85ml/3fl oz cold water
dripping, for greasing

Serves 6
Preparation: 15 minutes, plus 30 minutes' standing
Cooking: 1½–3 hours, plus 15 minutes' resting

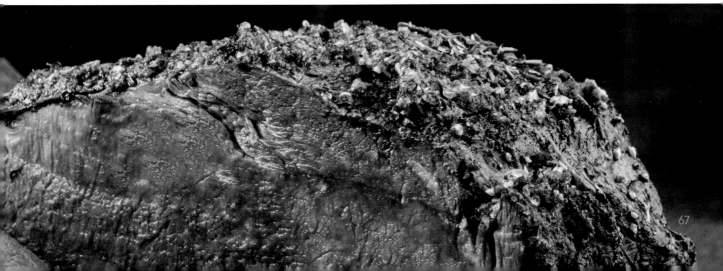

SAINT PATRICK

SAINT PATRICK
PATRON OF IRELAND (+461)
FEAST DAY: 17 MARCH

Patrick was captured when a boy by sea pirates and sold to an Irish druid. After six years he escaped and fled to Tours in France, where Saint Martin had founded a monastery twenty-five years earlier. In 431 Pope Celestine sent Patrick back to Ireland to preach the Christian faith.

According to legend, Saint Patrick founded 365 churches in Ireland, one for each day of the year.

You will be pleased to know that there are no snakes in this recipe as Saint Patrick chased them all out of Ireland. However, the bowl should be garnished with a shamrock, as this was the three-leaved symbol Saint Patrick used to explain to his people the mystery of the Triune God, the Holy Trinity.

The illustration shows Saint Patrick holding a shamrock in his right hand.

IRISH STEW

1. Trim any excess fat from the lamb. Heat the oil in a flameproof casserole, add the lamb and brown on all sides. Remove from the pan.
2. Add the onions to the casserole and cook for 5 minutes until browned. Return the lamb to the pan with the stock and water. Season to taste with salt and pepper. Bring to the boil, then reduce the heat, cover and simmer for 1 hour.
3. Add the carrots, potatoes, leeks and barley to the pan with the thyme, cover again, and simmer for a further hour.
4. Leave the stew to settle for a few minutes. Remove the fat from the liquid with a ladle, then pour off the liquid into a clean saucepan. Bring to a simmer over a medium heat and stir in the butter, then the parsley. Season well with salt and pepper and pour back into the casserole.
5. Serve with Savoy cabbage and potatoes.

Serves 4

Preparation: 10 minutes

Cooking: 2½ hours

1.5kg/3lb 5oz lean middle neck of lamb

1 tbsp vegetable oil

3 large onions, quartered

1 lamb stock cube

850ml/1½ pints water

4 large carrots, thickly sliced

4 large firm potatoes, cut into chunks

2 leeks, sliced

2 tbsp pearl barley

1 large thyme sprig

15g/½oz butter

1 tbsp chopped fresh parsley

salt and freshly ground black pepper

steamed Savoy cabbage and boiled jacket potatoes, to serve

VEGETABLES

SAINT
SAINT BARTHOLOMEW

SAINT BARTHOLOMEW (+C.71)
FEAST DAY: 24 AUGUST

Bartholomew was one of the Twelve Apostles, but is otherwise unknown. He is sometimes identified with Nathanael (see John 1:45–51), but scholars disagree.

Legend has it that he spread the Good News in Phrygia, Persia, Mesopotamia and even India, and that he was martyred by being skinned alive. Artists (including Michelangelo) have represented him holding his skin in one hand and a knife in the other.

He is revered as the patron saint of all who use knives and hence of all vegetables that grow in gardens, including cabbages and cauliflowers.

The picture shows Bartholomew amongst the trees while working in the garden.

CAULIFLOWER IN ORANGE SAUCE

1. Put the cauliflower florets into a saucepan with the stock, bring to the boil and cook for 5–10 minutes until tender but still crisp. Drain well, reserving the stock.
2. Melt the butter in a small saucepan, add the flour and cook for 1 minute, stirring vigorously. Remove the pan from the heat and gradually stir in the reserved stock, orange juice and salt and pepper to taste. Bring to the boil, stirring, and cook for 1–2 minutes until the sauce thickens.
3. Place the cauliflower in a warmed serving dish and pour over the sauce. Sprinkle with paprika, if liked, and serve immediately.

1 large cauliflower, divided into florets
300ml/10fl oz ham stock or water
25g/1oz butter
2 tbsp plain flour
3 tbsp orange juice
salt and freshly ground pepper
paprika (optional), for sprinkling

Serves 4–6
Preparation: 5 minutes
Cooking: 20–25 minutes

SAINT
SAINT BRIDGET (BIRGITTA) OF SWEDEN

SAINT BRIDGET OF SWEDEN (+1373)
FEAST DAY: 23 JULY

Bridget must have eaten a lot of swedes during her lifetime because the Swedish turnip was popular in Sweden before being introduced into Ireland and Britain. She would have needed sustenance for her long pilgrimages to Compostela, Rome and the Holy Land. It was during her travels that she received the divine visions that she wrote up as her Revelations. She founded the order of nuns named after her, the Bridgettines. She is patron of pilgrims. One of her sayings was, 'Who wouldn't love God who loves us so much!'

If you travel to the beautiful Bavarian State Library in Munich, you can find a wonderful woodcut of St Bridget of Sweden in which she is shown surrounded by pomegranates (swedes would not have been so artistic), symbolising the abundance of grace in the Resurrection. In that woodcut, Bridget is having a vision of Jesus and Mary as she writes the rules for her new monastery of Altomünster (Mariaminster), where the original monastery had been founded by Saint Alto (+760 – feastday 9 February), also shown.

MASHED SWEDE WITH ONIONS

1. Peel the swede and cut it into 2.5 cm/1 inch chunks. Bring a medium-sized saucepan of water to the boil, add the stock cube, swede and onion and bring back to the boil. Reduce the heat, cover and simmer for 15 minutes, or until the swede is tender when pierced with a skewer.
2. Drain and return to the pan. Add the cream and nutmeg and season well with salt and pepper. Mash with a potato masher until almost smooth. Alternatively, purée in a food processor.
3. Serve in a warmed serving dish topped with a knob of butter and a little nutmeg.

450g/1lb swede
1 pork stock cube
1 onion, chopped
4 tbsp single or double cream
generous pinch of freshly grated nutmeg, plus extra to garnish
salt and freshly ground black pepper
knob of butter, to serve

Serves 4
Preparation: 10 minutes
Cooking: 25 minutes

Photographs: Nataly Studio; Richard M Lee; Khumthong; Kyselova Inna / Shutterstock

SAINT FOY

SAINT FOY (+304)
FEAST DAY: 6 OCTOBER

Saint Foy has been chosen to bless this recipe for two reasons: the first is that the holy martyr went to heaven after being roasted (in the illustration the dove is descending with her crown).

The second is not so obvious: in the early Middle Ages every self-respecting town possessed relics, which brought both spiritual and economic status. These were kept in the monastery around which the town had developed. In the case of Conques (in the south of France) the relics of Saint Vincentius were revered in the monastery, but then removed by the authorities for another church. The monks devised a plan to replace them with another set. They knew that the relics of Saint Foy were kept in Agen, 200 kilometres away, so a monk named Arviscus was infiltrated into the community of Agen. After several years he was held in such repute that he was appointed guardian of the precious shrine. Waiting for the Feast of the Epiphany when the community, well dined and wined, had retired to sleep, Arviscus drilled a hole in the shrine and extracted the relics, which he put into a potato bag and brought back to his monastery, where they can still be venerated in the Abbey Church of Saint Foy.

ROAST POTATOES

1. Preheat the oven to 220°C/425°F/Gas 7. Cut the potatoes into even-sized pieces and place them in a large saucepan. Cover with cold water, add a little salt and bring to the boil. Cook for about 6 minutes. Drain well using a colander, then shake to fluff up the edges of the potatoes.
2. Meanwhile, heat the goose fat in a large tin in the preheated oven for about 5 minutes until piping hot. Add the potatoes, spooning the fat over them to coat, and shake the tin to prevent sticking. Roast for about 1 hour, depending on size, turning the potatoes from time to time, until golden and crisp. Sprinkle with salt just before serving.

1.4kg/3lb potatoes, such as Desiree, King Edward or Maris Piper, peeled
3 - 4 tbsp goose fat
salt

Serves 8
Preparation: 10–15 minutes
Cooking: 1 to 1¼ hours

Photograph: Nitr / Shutterstock

SAINT
SAINT MARK

SAINT MARK (+1ST CENTURY)
FEAST DAY: 25 APRIL

Saint Mark, revered as the first evangelist, begins his Gospel – in Greek 'eu' (good) 'angelion' (news) – with the words. 'The beginning of the good news'. He alone recounts how, when Jesus was arrested, 'he was followed by a young man with nothing on but a linen cloth. The soldiers caught hold of him, but he left the cloth in their hands and ran away naked' (14:51–52). Some think Mark was referring here to himself. Perhaps that is why when Jacob Jordaens painted the four Gospel writers the young man in the white cloth represents Mark, with the other three looking over his shoulder to be inspired by what he wrote first.

The link with the pumpkin comes from the date of his feast and an old Dutch saying:

Sowed on Saint Mark's before the sun
will give a pumpkin like a tun.

SPICY STUFFED PUMPKIN

1. Preheat the oven to 180°C/350°F/Gas 4. Cut the top off the pumpkin using a large sharp knife and reserve. Scrape out the seeds and stringy area with a large spoon and discard. Remove as much of the pumpkin flesh as possible and chop finely.
2. Mix the pumpkin flesh with all the remaining ingredients, except the oil, and spoon into the pumpkin shell.
3. Place the lid on top, smear with oil and place in a roasting tin. Roast in the preheated oven for 45–60 minutes until the pumpkin feels tender when tested with a skewer.

1.7–2kg/3½–4lb pumpkin
500g/1lb 2oz blanched and drained spinach, chopped
1 small red pepper, finely chopped
250g/8oz soft, medium-fat white cheese (curd cheese or grated mozzarella)
2.5 cm/1 inch piece fresh ginger, chopped
1 large garlic clove, crushed
2 tbsp ground mace
1 tsp ground cinnamon
½ tsp cayenne pepper
2 tsp caster sugar
large pinch of sea salt
oil, for greasing

Serves 4
Preparation: 30 minutes
Cooking: 45–60 minutes

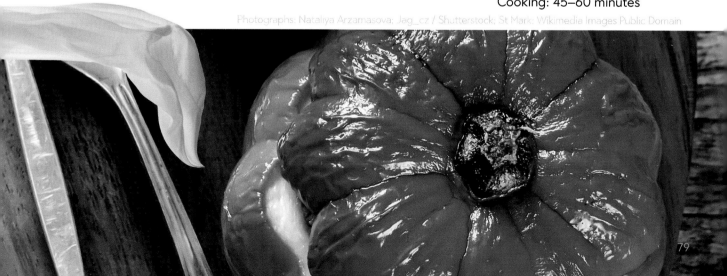

SAINT MARS

SAINT MARS (+530)
FEAST DAY: 13 APRIL

Saint Mars has only a slight connection with marrows, but a story told by the great historian Gregory of Tours (+594) provides the link.

While Mars was abbot of a monastery in Clermont-Ferrand in central France, a thief broke through the hedge into the vegetable garden one night and filled a sack with onions, fruit and marrows. But when he wanted to leave he could not find the gap he had made in the hedge. He became more and more anxious, fearful of the consequences if he were caught. Dawn came and the monks assembled for office in the church. Abbot Mars saw in a vision of what had happened in the vegetable garden and sent a monk to help the intruder. This man quickly made up a story about a lost cow, but the monk said to him, 'Calm down! The Abbot has seen you in a vision. He says you are to take your sack of vegetables this time, and not be so stupid in future. Go in peace!'

RECIPE
BUTTERED MARROW

1. Preheat the oven to 180°C/350°F/Gas 4. Cut the marrow into 1.5 cm/½ inch slices, then cut the slices in half.
2. Peel the slices with a potato peeler and remove the seeds.
3. Blanch in boiling water for 1 minute, then drain and place in a shallow dish.
4. Dot with butter, sprinkle with the nutmeg and salt and pepper to taste. Sprinkle over the chopped chilli, if using. Cover with foil and bake in the preheated oven for 20 minutes.
5. Remove from the oven and drain well before serving.

1 marrow, about 1kg/2lb 4oz
55g/2oz butter
large pinch of freshly grated nutmeg
1 chilli, deseeded and chopped (optional)
salt and freshly ground black pepper

Serves 4
Preparation: 10–15 minutes
Cooking: 20 minutes

Photograph: Romiri / Shutterstock

SAINT

SAINT MARTINA

SAINT MARTINA (+226)
FEAST DAY: 30 JANUARY

Saint Martina is revered as a Roman martyr. Well known for her charity to the poor, she was envied for her wealth and denounced as a Christian. She suffered torture and beheading. Those who executed her are said to have remarked, 'She may have belonged to the so-called weaker sex, but for strength of will she was of the strongest!'

Her name links her to Mars, usually remembered as the god of war, but originally venerated among the Romans as the god of agriculture. Hence the link with our recipe of vegetables.

But a special reason for asking her blessing is that her name is that of one of the two originators of this collection of recipes, Martina and Colette, both outstanding for their charity to the poor and for being strong willed.

SPICED WINTER VEGETABLES

1. Preheat the oven to 220°C/425°F/Gas 7. Bring a large saucepan of water to the boil.
2. Cut the parsnips and carrots into wedges of similar size. Add them to the saucepan and cook for 5 minutes. Drain thoroughly and place in an ovenproof dish with the onions, leeks and garlic. Pour over the oil, sprinkle in the spices and salt and pepper to taste, then mix until all the vegetables are well coated.
3. Roast in the preheated oven for at least 1 hour. Turn the vegetables from time to time until they are tender and starting to colour. Remove from the oven, transfer to a warmed serving dish and serve with meat or fish.

4 parsnips, scrubbed and trimmed, unpeeled

4 carrots, scrubbed and trimmed, unpeeled

2 onions, quartered

1 red onion, quartered

3 leeks, trimmed and cut into 6cm/2½ inch slices, white pieces only

2 garlic cloves, unpeeled and left whole

4 tbsp rapeseed oil

pinch of paprika

a little mixed spice

salt and freshly ground pepper

Serves 4
Preparation: 15 minutes
Cooking: 1 hour

Photograph: JoannaTkaczuk / Shutterstock

Bread in the bread basket in the dining room at Manresa.

SAINTLY FEASTS

BREADS

ABIGAIL

The choice of a holy person to accompany this recipe for a special bread is not difficult. The Old Testament (1 Samuel 25) provides the perfect figure: Abigail, as 'clever and beautiful' as her husband, Nabal, was 'surly and mean'. When King David asked this wealthy landowner for food for his men, he was turned away with insults. He swore to take deadly revenge. Fortunately Abigail was informed and at once 'hastily took two hundred loaves, two skins of wine ... five measures of roasted grain'; she loaded all these and more on donkeys and rode off to intercept David. 'As soon as Abigail saw David, she quickly dismounted from the donkey and, falling on her face in front of David, prostrated herself on the ground.' David was enchanted, so much so that when Nabal died a natural death not long afterwards, David 'sent and wooed Abigail, to make her his wife'.

The illustration (from a Dutch tile) shows Abigail kneeling before David with her food displayed before her.

SWEET POTATO & RAISIN BREAD

1. Preheat the oven to 180°C/350°F/Gas 4. Grease a 23 x 13 cm/9 x 5 inch loaf tin.
2. Sift the flour, baking powder, salt, cinnamon and nutmeg into a small bowl. Set aside.
3. Using an electric mixer, beat the sweet potatoes with the sugar, butter and eggs until well mixed.
4. Add the flour mixture and the raisins. Stir with a wooden spoon until the flour is just mixed in.
5. Transfer the batter to the prepared tin and bake in the preheated oven for 1–1¼ hours, or until a skewer inserted into the centre comes out clean.
6. Transfer to a wire rack in the tin and leave to cool for 15 minutes, then turn out onto the rack and leave to cool completely.

butter or margarine, for greasing

225–275g/8–9¾oz self-raising flour

2 tsp baking powder

½ tsp salt

1 tsp ground cinnamon

½ tsp grated nutmeg

450g/1lb mashed cooked sweet potatoes

85g/3oz light brown sugar

115g/4oz butter or margarine, melted and cooled

3 eggs, beaten

85g/3oz raisins or sultanas

Makes 1 loaf
Preparation: 15 minutes
Cooking: 1–1¼ hours, plus cooling

SAINT AUGUSTINE

SAINT AUGUSTINE (+430)
FEAST DAY: 28 AUGUST

Saint Augustine, the great theologian and Bishop of Hippo in North Africa, frequently refers to bread, as it could serve to teach his converts about the richness of the Eucharist. 'When the bread and the wine at the altar are made holy by the words of the priest, they are the Body and Blood of Our Lord Jesus Christ. That is the way the Lord Jesus wished to stay with us. When you receive it in the right way, it becomes you.' And he quotes Saint Paul, 'The bread that we break, is it not a sharing in the body of Christ? Because there is one bread, we who are many are one body.'
(I Corinthians 10:16–17)

The making of bread – the corn being ground, mixed with water and baked – shows us the need for repentance, but also symbolises both the unity that comes from the multiple ears of corn, and the role of the sacraments, as we become blessed with the water of baptism and the fire of the Spirit in confirmation.

COURGETTE TEA BREAD

1. Preheat the oven to 180°C/350°F/Gas 4.
2. Line the bottom and sides of a 23 x 13 cm /9 x inch loaf tin with baking paper and grease the paper.
3. Put the butter into a saucepan over a low heat and heat until melted. Set aside.
4. Using an electric mixer, beat together the eggs and oil until thick. Beat in the sugar. Stir in the melted butter and courgettes. Set aside.
5. In a separate bowl, sift all the dry ingredients together three times. Carefully fold into the courgette mixture. Fold in the sultanas.
6. Pour the batter into the prepared tin and bake in the preheated oven for 1 hour–1 hour 10 minutes, or until a skewer inserted into the centre comes out clean. Leave to cool in the tin for 10 minutes, then turn out onto a wire rack and leave to cool completely.

55g/2oz butter

3 eggs

225ml/8fl oz vegetable oil

300g/10½oz caster sugar

2 unpeeled courgettes, grated

280g/10oz plain flour

2 tsp bicarbonate of soda

1 tsp baking powder

½ tsp salt

1 tsp ground cinnamon

1 tsp grated nutmeg

¼ tsp ground cloves

115g/4oz sultanas

Makes 1 loaf
Preparation: 15–20 minutes
Cooking: 1 hour–1 hour 10
 minutes, plus cooling

Photograph: Timolina / Shutterstock

SAINT CONRAD OF PARZHAM

SAINT CONRAD OF PARZHAM (+1894)
FEAST DAY: 21 APRIL

Saint Conrad, better known in Germany as 'Bruder Kuno', spent forty-one years as the porter of the Capuchin friary in Altötting, site of a popular Marian shrine. His early life was on a farm, but when his parents died, he left everything to follow the Franciscan life.

He is shown with a loaf of bread in his left hand and his right hand blessing a child he is helping. Despite his modest role in life, he became famous for his boundless love of those in need, for whom he constantly found food, and also for his intense life of prayer. People who knew him said that you could see that the Lord was with him.

BROWN SODA BREAD

1. Lightly grease a baking sheet. Preheat the oven to 190°C/375°F/Gas 5.
2. Sift all the dry ingredients into a large bowl, tipping in any bran left in the sieve.
3. Slowly add enough buttermilk to make a soft dough. You may not need it all.
4. Knead the dough lightly until smooth, then transfer to the prepared baking sheet and shape into a large round about 5cm/2in thick.
5. Use a sharp knife to make a large cross on the top of the dough. Sprinkle over a little extra wholemeal flour and bake in the preheated oven for 40–50 minutes until risen and firm. Leave to cool on the baking sheet for 5 minutes before transferring to a wire rack.
6. Cover the bread with a damp (not wet) cloth and leave to cool.

butter or margarine, for greasing

450g/1lb self-raising white flour

450g/1lb self-raising wholemeal flour, plus extra for sprinkling

2 tsp salt

1 tsp bicarbonate of soda

2 tsp caster sugar

850ml/1½ pints buttermilk, skimmed milk or yogurt

Makes 1 loaf

Preparation: 10–15 minutes

Cooking: 40–50 minutes, plus cooling

Tip:
Don't be tempted to double up on the wholemeal flour and omit the white flour – it may seem like a healthy option, but the result will be heavy and dense.

Photograph: Joerg Beuge / Shutterstock

SAINT

SAINT JOHN

SAINT JOHN THE APOSTLE
(+2ND CENTURY)
FEAST DAY: 27 DECEMBER

Saint John was also celebrated in earlier centuries on 6 May, hence the German saying, 'Johannisnacht gesteckte Zwiebel/wird gross fast wie ein Butterkübel' ('The onion planted on Saint John's night/ soon grows fat as a butter blob'). That provides our justification for linking his name with this recipe, which contains onions. The feast was kept because of the supposed torture inflicted on Saint John in Rome: he was plunged into a pot of boiling oil (as shown in this illustration), but emerged unscathed.

The recipe also contains rosemary, a symbol of fragrant friendship, and here Saint John deserves mention as he is known as the 'beloved disciple', the intimate friend of Jesus.

RED ONION & ROSEMARY LOAF

1. Preheat the oven to 160°C/325°F/Gas 3 and line a 23 x 13 cm/9 x 5 inch loaf tin with baking paper.
2. Fry the onions in the oil for 10 minutes or until softened and starting to caramelise. Set aside and leave to cool.
3. Sift the flour and baking powder with a little salt into a mixing bowl, then add the butter and eggs.
4. Using an electric mixer beat the mixture for 4 minutes, or until smooth.
5. Fold in the onions and rosemary, then scrape the batter into the prepared tin.
6. Bake in the preheated oven for 55 minutes, or until a skewer inserted into the centre of the cake comes out clean.
7. Transfer to a wire rack in the tin and leave to cool for 10 minutes, then turn out onto the rack and leave to cool completely before serving.

3 red onions, sliced
2 tbsp olive oil
300g/10½oz self-raising flour
2 tsp baking powder
250g/9oz butter, softened
4 large eggs
2 tbsp rosemary leaves
salt

Makes 1 loaf
Preparation: 15 minutes
Cooking: 55 minutes, plus 10 minutes cooling

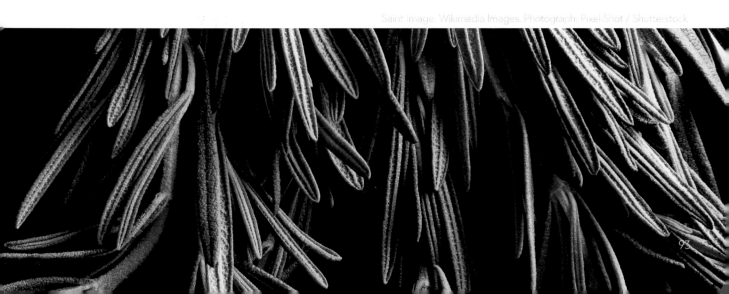

SAINT MARTIAL

SAINT MARTIAL (+250)
FEAST DAY: 30 JUNE

Although Saint Martial is venerated as the first bishop of the city of Limoges in France, almost nothing of historical interest about him can be found. However, this did not prevent the growth of a wonderful series of legends.

His birth was pushed back into the time of Christ and he became not only a disciple of Saint Peter – who duly appointed him a bishop – but he also served at the Last Supper. Imagination went further: he was a Benjamite, like Saint Paul (Philippians 3:4–6), but more important for our purposes is that he was the boy mentioned by John who happened to have the five loaves of bread handy for the feeding of the five thousand (John 6:9). The image of him here is derived from one of the mosaics at Ravenna.

RECIPE

SAGE SODA BREAD

1. Preheat the oven to 220°C/425°F/Gas 7. Grease a baking sheet.
2. Sift the dry ingredients into a mixing bowl. Stir in the sage and gradually add enough buttermilk to make a soft dough.
3. Shape the dough into a round with your hands and place on the prepared baking sheet.
4. Cut a deep cross in the top of the round and bake in the preheated oven for about 40 minutes until the loaf is well risen and sounds hollow when tapped on the base. Transfer to a wire rack and leave to cool, covered with a damp (not wet) tea towel.

oil, for greasing

175g/6oz self-raising white flour

115g/4oz self-raising wholemeal flour

½ tsp salt

1 tsp bicarbonate of soda

2 tbsp chopped fresh sage or 2 tsp dried sage

300–450ml/10–16fl oz buttermilk or yogurt

Makes 1 loaf
Preparation: 10 mins
Cooking: 40 mins, plus cooling

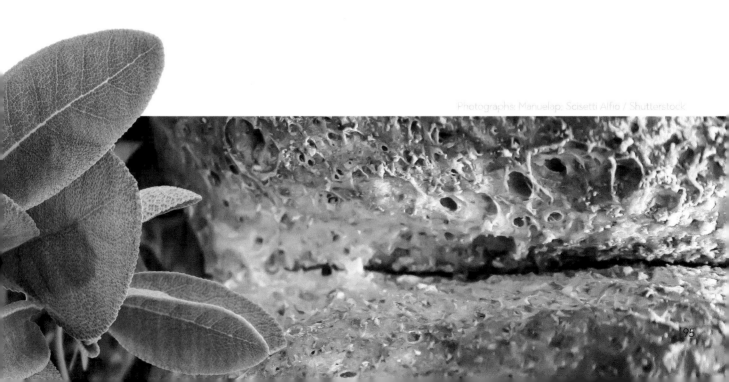

SAINT MEINGOLD

SAINT MEINGOLD OF HUY (+892)
FEAST DAY: 8 FEBRUARY

Saint Meingold can be linked with this recipe thanks to a mispronunciation of his name: 'mangold', which suggests 'mango'. The stories that grew up around him are equally tenuous, but they provide another link: bread.

Curiously enough, Saint Meingold is the patron of bakers. The reason for this is far from clear. There was a Count of Huy called Meingold, who was murdered with his wife by a brother-in-law envious of their wealth, which may have come partly from their bakeries. But the Belgian town of Huy had loved them for their generosity and kept a shrine (illustrated) in memory of Saint Meingold. The fact that his head is missing adds to the aura of mystery around this saintly man.

MANGO TEA BREAD

1. Preheat the oven to 180°C/350°F/Gas 4. Line a 23 x 13 cm/9 x 5 inch loaf tin with baking paper and grease the paper.
2. Sift together the flour, bicarbonate of soda, cinnamon and salt. Set aside.
3. Using an electric mixer, cream the butter until soft.
4. Beat in the eggs and sugar until pale and fluffy. Beat in the oil.
5. Fold the dry ingredients into the creamed ingredients in batches.
6. Fold in the mango, two-thirds of the coconut and the raisins.
7. Spoon the batter into the prepared tin.
8. Sprinkle over the remaining coconut. Bake in the preheated oven for 50–60 minutes, or until a skewer inserted into the centre of the loaf comes out clean. Leave to cool in the tin for 10 minutes, then turn out onto a wire rack and leave to cool completely.

280g/10oz plain flour

2 tsp bicarbonate of soda

2 tsp ground cinnamon

½ tsp salt

115g/4oz butter or margarine, at room temperature, plus extra for greasing

3 large eggs, at room temperature

300g/10½oz golden caster sugar

125ml/4fl oz vegetable oil

1 large ripe mango, peeled and chopped

90g/3¼oz desiccated coconut

70g/2½oz raisins or sultanas

Makes 1 loaves
Preparation: 20 minutes
Cooking: 50–60 minutes, plus cooling

SAINT
SAINT NONNOSUS

SAINT NONNOSUS (+575)
FEAST DAY: 2 SEPTEMBER

We are told, by no less an authority than Saint Gregory the Great (pope at the start of the 7th century), that Saint Nonnosus was a pious monk at the San Silvestre monastery on Monte Soratte near Rome. The stories about him need to be taken with a pinch of salt, but one of them links him firmly to the olives in this recipe.

At one time the monastery was running very short of olive oil, and its olive groves were almost bereft of olives. The abbot suggested that the monks should go and beg for oil from their neighbours. Nonnosus demurred: 'Our neighbours have the same problem as ourselves. No, just collect the few olives that are on the trees and bring them to me.' He then had the olives pressed and the tiny amount of oil that came out went into a small jar. Nonnosus placed this on the altar and spent the night in prayer. Next morning he told the monks to pour a few drops of the oil into each of the large empty olive jars belonging to the monastery, and to close them up while he returned to his prayers. The next morning, all the jars were full to the brim.

The illustration is derived from the image of Saint Gregory, the biographer of Saint Nonnosus, painted on the ceiling of the church of Saint Luzia in Eschfeld, Eifel, Germany, by the pastor, Christoph März, c.1920.

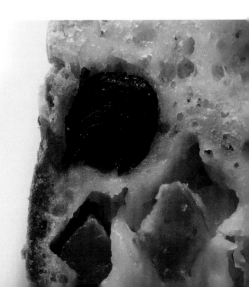

OLIVE, MUSHROOM & HAM LOAF

1. Preheat the oven to 180°C/350°F/Gas 4 and line a large loaf tin with non-stick baking paper.
2. Sift the flour and baking powder into a mixing bowl and add the butter and eggs.
3. Using an electric mixer, beat the mixture for 4 minutes, or until smooth and well whipped.
4. Fold in the olives, mushrooms and ham, then scrape the mixture into the prepared tin.
5. Bake in the preheated oven for 55 minutes, or until a skewer inserted into the centre of the loaf comes out clean.
6. Leave to cool in the tin for 10 minutes, then turn out onto a wire rack and leave to cool completely.

300g/10½oz self-raising flour
2 tsp baking powder
250g/9oz butter, softened
4 large eggs
70g/2½oz green olives, stoned and halved
50g/1¾oz mushrooms, diced
70g/2½oz cooked ham, cubed

Makes 1 loaf
Preparation: 20 minutes
Cooking: 55 minutes, plus cooling

SAINT DAVID

SAINT DAVID, PATRON OF WALES

(+601)

FEAST DAY: 1 MARCH

Saint David is the obvious saint to bless this typical Welsh bread. Nearly all that is known of him comes from unhistorical legends. He is said to have been an uncle of King Arthur (also 6th century) and trained by Saint Paulinus of York. After years of living as a hermit, he founded the monastery of Mynyw (Menevia, now Saint David's).

Famous for his ascetic life, David practised much penance, and would recite by heart all 150 Psalms every day, pausing to kneel between each Psalm; he never drank alcohol and was nicknamed Aquaticus (Waterman). However, when the monastery ran short of altar wine, the monks were able to draw wine from the well David opened for them. Another miracle attributed to him occurred while he was on pilgrimage to the Holy Land: like the Apostles at Pentecost he could speak all the languages of those he met. His cult was officially recognised by Pope Callixtus II in 1120, who declared that two pilgrimages to his grave were the equivalent of one to Rome.

WELSH BARA BRITH

1. Put the raisins, sultanas and currants into a bowl and add the tea. Leave to soak overnight and then drain well.
2. Preheat the oven to 180°C/350°F/Gas 4. Line a 30 x 13 cm/12 x 5 inch loaf tin with baking paper.
3. Put the eggs, sugar and salt into a large bowl and beat together until foamy. Sift in the flour, baking powder and mixed spice and fold into the mixture. Fold in the drained fruit and spread the batter smoothly in the prepared loaf tin.
4. Bake in the preheated oven for about 1 hour. Cover with foil to prevent the top burning and bake for a further 30–45 minutes. Leave to cool in the tin for 5 minutes before turning out onto a wire rack. Brush with clear honey while still hot and leave to cool completely.

200g/7oz raisins
100g/3½oz sultanas
100g/3½oz currants
225ml/8fl oz cold black tea
2 eggs
55g/2oz demerara sugar
pinch of salt
400g/14oz plain flour
3 tsp baking powder
1 tsp mixed spice or ground
   cinnamon
clear honey, for glazing

Makes 1 loaf
Preparation: 10 minutes, plus
   overnight soaking
Cooking: 1 hour 30 minutes to
   1 hour 45 minutes, plus cooling

Photograph: MShev / Shutterstock

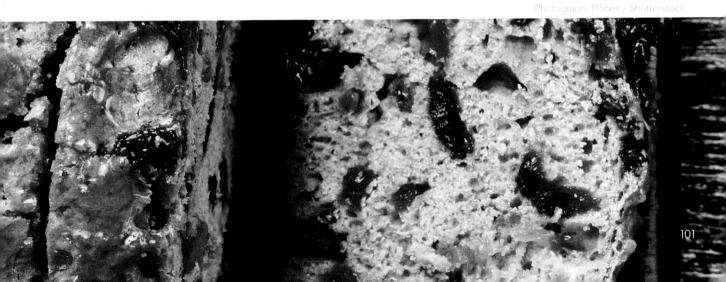

SAINTLY FEASTS

CAKES

SAINT ADELBERT OF EGMOND

SAINT ADELBERT (+741)
FEAST DAY: 25 JUNE

The life (largely legendary) of Saint Adelbert claims that he came from a royal Scottish family. He became a monk and joined Saint Willibrord when he went to spread the faith in Frisia in the Low Countries. He settled in the village of Egmond, near the coast in what is now North Holland, where he preached to the pagans and eradicated idolatry – thus becoming a Dutch hero. Eventually he was ordained an archdeacon.

Adelbert's link with apples comes from a story about a meal with his good friend, Eggo, and family. When he announced that he had to leave them, they asked sadly if they would ever see him again. Adelbert took the seeds of an apple he was eating and flung them on the ground, declaring, 'When a tree has grown from these seeds, I will be back!'

RECIPE
DUTCH APPLE CAKE

1. Preheat the oven to 180°C/350°F/Gas 4. Grease a 20 cm/8 inch round cake tin and line the base with baking paper.
2. Sift the flour, salt and sugar together into a mixing bowl, then rub in the butter with your fingertips.
3. Make a well in the centre and add the milk in a steady stream, stirring with a fork to incorporate the flour. Transfer the mixture to the prepared tin and pat level, making sure it is pushed well into the edges and against the sides of the tin.
4. Arrange the apple slices in a circular pattern to cover the top of the cake, pressing the thin edges into the dough.
5. Brush with melted butter or margarine, sprinkle with cinnamon and sugar, and bake in the preheated oven for 55 minutes. Serve warm, cut into wedges.

275g/9¾oz self-raising flour

½ tsp salt

1 tbsp caster sugar

125g/4½oz butter or margarine, plus extra for greasing

125ml/4fl oz milk

2 Granny Smith apples, peeled, cored and thinly sliced

Topping

25g/1oz butter, melted

1 tsp ground cinnamon or mixed spice

2 tbsp caster sugar

Serves 8

Preparation: 20 minutes

Cooking: 55 minutes

SAINT CLEMENS

SAINT CLEMENS (+1820)
(CLEMENS MARIA HOFBAUER CSsR)
FEAST DAY: 15 DECEMBER

The cathedral of Vienna is dedicated to Saint Stephen, but the locals have a special reverence for another patron, known as the Apostle of Vienna. His name deserves to be attached to the archetypal cake of the city for a special reason.

Saint Clemens was born in 1751 in Moravia. His father, Pavel Dvorák, was a Czech who changed his name to the German Hofbauer. On the early death of his father, the boy had to learn a trade and became a baker. He soon became famous for his generous help to the poor, but his love of prayer led him to live for a while as a hermit. Eventually he joined the Redemptorist Congregation. He was sent to work in Warsaw and did his best to help a population ravaged by the Napoleonic wars. Exiled in 1808, Clemens went to Vienna where he became famous for his original pastoral work: spending time with students and intellectuals of the highest classes, while also visiting people in their homes and in hospitals and caring for the hungry, where his skill as a baker served him well.

Clemens is the patron saint of hopeless cases.

SACHERTORTE
(FOR CHOCOLATE LOVERS!)

1. Preheat the oven to 180°C/350°F/Gas 4. Lightly grease a 23 cm/9 inch round cake tin and line with baking paper. Put the chocolate into a heatproof bowl set over a saucepan of simmering water and heat until melted. Stir in the water and leave to cool. Put the butter and sugar into a mixing bowl and beat until pale and fluffy. Beat in the egg yolks, one at a time, beating well between each addition. Stir in the melted chocolate, then the flour.

2. In a clean, grease-free bowl, whisk the egg whites until stiff peaks hold, then whisk in the remaining sugar. Fold into the chocolate mixture and spoon into the prepared tin. Bake in the preheated oven for 30 minutes until firm. Leave to cool in the tin for 5 minutes, then turn out onto a wire rack and leave to cool completely. Leave the cake upside down.

3. To decorate, split the cold cake in two horizontally and place one half on a serving plate. Heat the jam and rub through a fine sieve. Brush half the jam onto one layer of the cake, then cover with the remaining cake layer and brush with the remaining jam. Leave to stand at room temperature for 1 hour, or until the jam has set.

4. Put the plain chocolate and the butter into a heatproof bowl set over a saucepan of simmering water and heat until the chocolate has melted. Stir occasionally until smooth, then leave to thicken. Use to cover the cake.

5. Put the milk chocolate into a heatproof bowl set over a saucepan of simmering water and heat until melted. Place in a small greaseproof piping bag and snip a small hole at the tip. Pipe 'Sacher' with a large 'S' onto the top of the cake. Leave to set at room temperature. You could use vanilla icing instead, it will set well and will look good on the dark chocolate.

vegetable oil, for greasing

150g/5½oz plain chocolate

1 tbsp water

150g/5½oz unsalted butter, softened

125g/4½oz caster sugar, plus 2 tbsp

2 large eggs, separated

150g/5½oz plain flour, sifted

To decorate

225g/8oz apricot jam

125g/4½oz plain chocolate, chopped

125g/4½oz unsalted butter

25g/1oz milk chocolate

Serves 10–12

Preparation: 30–40 minutes

Cooking: 30 minutes in oven, plus cooling

Photographs: lauradibi; Charlie's / Shutterstock

SAINT HUMPHREY

SAINT HUMPHREY (+400)
FEAST DAY: 12 JUNE

Saint Humphrey is known in the East by the Greek form of his name, Onuphrius, although he may have been an Abyssinian prince who spent his life as a hermit in the Egyptian desert.

A legend about his time as a young novice recounts that out of devotion to the child Jesus sitting on the lap of his mother, he offered to share his daily bread with Jesus, and Jesus accepted. As an adult, Humphrey left the monastery and lived for sixty years in complete poverty, dispensing with clothes: his long beard and abundant body hair covered his modesty. A white deer kept him supplied with milk, and his diet of dates, collected from a palm tree near his cell (he can be seen plucking dates in the illustration) justifies the choice of his name for this recipe.

Photographs: Nataly Studio; Pixfiction; SMarina / Shutterstock

BANANA, DATE & CHERRY LOAF

1. Preheat the oven to 180°C/350°F/Gas 4. Grease a 900g/2lb loaf tin and line with greased baking paper.
2. Mash the bananas in a large bowl. Dissolve the bicarbonate of soda in the milk, then add to the bananas with the remaining ingredients and mix very thoroughly for 2–3 minutes.
3. Pour the batter into the prepared tin, smooth the top and bake in the preheated oven for 1–1¼ hours or until the loaf is well risen and golden brown.
4. Turn out of the tin, remove the paper and leave to cool on a wire rack. Serve just as it is or spread with butter.

2 large ripe bananas

1 tsp bicarbonate of soda

2 tbsp boiling milk

100g/3½oz butter or margarine, plus extra for greasing

175g/6oz caster sugar

2 eggs, beaten

225g/8oz plain flour

1 tsp baking powder

55g/2oz glacé cherries, chopped

55g/2oz stoned dates, chopped

Makes 1 loaf
Preparation: 15 minutes
Cooking: 1–1¼ hours

SAINT POMPONIUS

SAINT POMPONIUS (+536)
FEAST DAY: 30 APRIL

The link of this recipe with Saint Pomponius comes through an accident of sound. A courgette is a little pumpkin. In Dutch the word for a pumpkin is pompoen (pronounced 'pompoon'), and that is what Dutch people think of when they hear the name of this saint.

In fact the saint was blessed with the name of an ancient Latin family, the *Pomponia gens*, which counted among its members an admiral of Julius Caesar and the wife of Cicero. Pomponius was Bishop of Naples (508–36) and founded the original church of Santa Maria Maggiore (now completely rebuilt) in that city. He remained a staunch opponent of Arianism even at the time of the Ostrogoth King Theodoric, who had imprisoned Pope John I. The latter wrote a letter from prison praising Pomponius, who was buried in his own church and is still venerated.

COURGETTE CAKE

1. Preheat the oven to 180°C/350°F/Gas 4. Lightly grease a 20 cm/8 inch round cake tin and line the base with baking paper.
2. Place the eggs and sugar in a large mixing bowl and whisk until very pale and thick.
3. Fold in the courgettes. Carefully fold in the flour. Drizzle over the melted butter and fold in.
4. Pour the batter into the prepared tin and bake in the preheated oven for 25–35 minutes, or until springy to the touch. Leave to cool in the tin for 5 minutes, then transfer to a wire rack and leave to cool completely.
5. To make the frosting, beat together all the ingredients until just combined. Spread over the top of the cake, cut into wedges and serve.

butter, for greasing
3 eggs
85g/3oz golden caster sugar
150g/5½oz self-raising flour
225g/8oz courgettes, grated
25g/1oz butter, melted

Frosting
175g/6oz full-fat cream cheese
1 tbsp lemon or orange juice
85g/3oz icing sugar

Serves 8
Preparation: 20–25 minutes
Cooking: 25–35 minutes, plus cooling

SAINT SYMEON
THE HOLY FOOL

SAINT SYMEON (+530)
FEAST DAY: 1 JULY

In the Eastern Churches the phenomenon of the 'holy fool' is well established, and one of the most famous, Saint Symeon, provides a useful link with walnuts.

Symeon (from Emesa, today Homs in Syria) took Saint Paul's words, 'God has chosen the fools to shame the wise' (1 Corinthians 1:27) very literally. He played the fool to hide his holiness and to convert the world's 'wise'. On one occasion he dragged a dead dog behind him into the city, with children running behind him calling him a fool. On the next day, a Sunday, he entered a church, put out the lights and threw nuts at the women. But the people leaving the church listened to him when he cried out against sin, and many were converted. The alms he collected went to feed the poor, and his biographer points out how closely Symeon was imitating Christ.

WALNUT PUMPKIN LOAF

1. Preheat the oven to 180°C/350°F/Gas 4. Grease a 23 x13 cm/9 x 5 inch loaf tin and line with baking paper.
2. Loosely combine the pumpkin and banana with a fork and set aside.
3. Sift the flour, salt, baking powder, bicarbonate of soda and mixed spice into a mixing bowl and set aside.
4. In a separate large bowl cream the butter and sugar until smooth. Add the honey and egg, mixing until the mixture becomes loose. Add the pumpkin and banana mixture.
5. Stir in the flour mixture in three additions, adding the walnuts just as the flour is combined. Do not over-mix.
6. Pour the batter into the prepared tin and bake in the preheated oven for 45–50 minutes until risen and firm to the touch and a skewer inserted into the centre of the loaf comes out clean. Leave to cool in the tin for 5 minutes, then turn out onto a wire rack and leave to cool completely.

300g/10½oz pumpkin, peeled, deseeded and grated

1 large banana, mashed

375g/13oz plain flour

¼ tsp salt

2 tsp baking powder

½ tsp bicarbonate of soda

2 tsp mixed spice

175g/6oz butter or margarine, plus extra for greasing

125g/4½oz soft brown sugar

150g/5½oz clear honey

1 large egg

125g/4½oz chopped walnuts

Makes 1 loaf

Preparation: 25 minutes

Cooking: 45–50 minutes, plus cooling

MARY, QUEEN OF HEAVEN

MARY, QUEEN OF HEAVEN
FEAST DAY: 22 AUGUST

Mary, the mother of Jesus, is venerated with the title 'Queen' for a very simple reason: the entry of her Risen Son into heaven conferred on him the title of 'King', and the arrival of his mother, 'assumed' into heaven on her death, justified giving her the title. Very early in the history of the Church this was recognised; the medieval Latin hymn, 'Salve Regina', is one example, but the fifth Glorious Mystery of the Rosary repeats the theme. The feast is celebrated on 22 August, but at the insistence of Spanish-speaking believers, it was first celebrated on 31 May (closing the month dedicated to her memory). The date was moved by Pope Pius XII in 1954 when he proclaimed the Assumption, so that the feast of Mary, Queen of Heaven would coincide with the octave of 15 August.

QUEEN OF PUDDINGS

Variation: You can ring the changes with this old favourite by putting raspberries or blackberries in the base of the dish.

1. Mix together the breadcrumbs and granulated sugar. Put the milk into a saucepan, add the lemon rind and butter and heat gently until the butter melts, then pour the mixture over the breadcrumbs. Stir well and leave to swell for 30 minutes. Meanwhile, preheat the oven to 160°C/325°F/Gas 3 and grease an 850 ml/1½ pint ovenproof dish.
2. Beat the egg yolks and blend into the cooled breadcrumb mixture. Pour into the prepared dish.
3. Bake in the preheated oven for 30 minutes, or until firm and set. Warm the jam and spread over the pudding. Whisk the egg whites until stiff peaks hold. Sift and fork the caster sugar into the egg white and pile the mixture on top of the pudding. Stir or ruffle the top and dredge with caster sugar. Decorate with glacé cherries and angelica.
4. Return the pudding to the oven and bake for a further 30 minutes, or until crisp and golden. Serve hot or cold.

85g/3oz fresh white breadcrumbs

25g/1oz granulated sugar

450ml/15fl oz milk

2 tsp finely grated lemon rind

25g/1oz butter or margarine, plus extra for greasing

2 large eggs, separated

2 tbsp raspberry jam

55g/2oz caster sugar, plus extra for dredging

glacé cherries and angelica, to decorate

Serves 6
Preparation: 10–15 minutes
Cooking: 1 hour

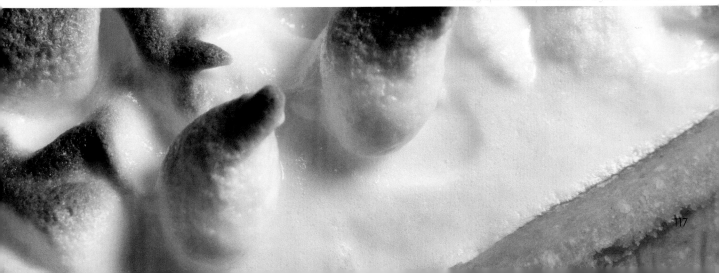

SAINT CLEMENT OF ROME

**SAINT CLEMENT (+ 1ST CENTURY)
FEAST DAY: 23 NOVEMBER**

Oranges and lemons,
Say the bells of St Clement's

Saint Clement is listed as a very early bishop of Rome. At least one Letter to the Corinthians was written by him, and he is venerated as the first 'Apostolic Father'. His pastoral work brought many noble Romans into the Church. His intervention in the disputes at Corinth is considered exemplary of the primacy of Rome. A later tradition claims that he was exiled to work in the mines in the Crimea, but as he continued to convert many he was condemned to be flung into the sea bound to an anchor (which figures in his left hand in the illustration).

Many churches are dedicated to Saint Clement, five of them in London. It is through them that our recipe finds a link with London, and then with the nursery rhyme that mentions lemons – the basic ingredient of lime marmalade.

LIME MARMALADE CHEESECAKE

1. Grease an 18–20 cm/7inch springform cake tin. Put the butter into a saucepan over a low heat and heat until melted. Stir in the biscuit crumbs. Press the mixture evenly over the base of the prepared tin. Chill while you make the filling,

2. Soften the cheese in a large mixing bowl. Beat in the egg yolks, 55g/2oz of the sugar, the lemon juice and rind, cream and marmalade.

3. Put the gelatine and water into a small heatproof bowl over a saucepan of hot water and stir until the gelatine has dissolved. Beat the gelatine into the cheese mixture. Set aside until the mixture is on the point of setting.

4. Whisk the egg whites until stiff peaks hold, then whisk in the remaining sugar. Fold lightly but thoroughly into the cheese mixture.

5. Spoon the mixture into the tin and shake gently to level the surface. Chill for 3–4 hours, or until the filling is set. Carefully release and remove the springform and lift the cheesecake out, keeping it on the base of the tin.

6. To make the topping, heat the marmalade over a low heat until it has a soft spreading consistency. Leave to cool slightly, then spread over the top and sides of the cheesecake. Coat the sides evenly with the nuts, then decorate with lime slices and mint.

55g/2oz butter or margarine, plus extra for greasing
115g/4oz gingernut biscuits, finely crushed

Filling
225g/8oz full-fat soft cheese
2 eggs, separated
115g/4oz caster sugar
juice and grated rind of 1 lemon
150ml/5fl oz double or whipping cream
4 tbsp lime marmalade
15g/½oz gelatine
4 tbsp water

Topping:
4 tbsp lime marmalade
55g/2oz chopped toasted nuts
slices of lime and a sprig of fresh mint to decorate

Serves 8
Preparation: 1 hour, plus setting and 3-4 hours chilling

SAINT EDITH STEIN

SAINT EDITH STEIN (+1942)
FEAST DAY: 9 AUGUST

Saint Edith came from a devout Jewish family. When she became a Christian, she decided eventually to enter a Carmelite convent, taking Sister Teresa Benedicta of the Cross as her name in religion. But first she attended the celebration of the Feast of Tabernacles with her mother, who found her daughter's decision very strange. 'Wasn't that a nice homily by our rabbi?' she said to Edith. 'Yes', Edith replied, 'as long as one doesn't know better!'

When the Nazi persecution of the Jews started in Germany she was moved to the Carmel at Echt, in the Netherlands. In 1942 she was arrested there by the Nazis and deported to Auschwitz, where she died in the gas chamber.

This depiction below of the Feast of Tabernacles links this recipe with the Jewish world and thus to Saint Edith Stein. For Jewish people, the citron is important as a symbol of the harvest and is used to celebrate the end of the harvest and the exodus of the Jewish people from Egypt into the Promised Land. The citron is a close relative of the lemon.

LEMON CURD & MANGO SPONGE PUDDING

1. Grease a 1.2 litre/2 pint pudding basin. Peel the mango. Cut off a cheek, slice and place in the base of the prepared basin. Dice the remaining mango flesh and put aside.
2. Using an electric mixer, beat together the butter, sugar, eggs, flour and baking powder.
3. Mix the diced mango and one third of the lemon curd into the batter. Spoon into the basin, cover with baking paper and foil and secure with string.
4. Place the basin in a large saucepan, pour in boiling water until it reaches halfway up the sides of the basin, cover and steam for 1½ hours.
5. Mix the remaining lemon curd with the crème fraîche in a small saucepan. Heat gently and serve with the sponge.

1 mango
150g/5½oz butter, plus extra for greasing
115g/4oz caster sugar
3 large eggs
175g/6oz self-raising flour, sifted
1 tsp baking powder
350g/12oz lemon curd
200g/7oz half-fat crème fraîche

Serves 6
Preparation: 15–20 minutes
Cooking: 1 hour 30 minutes

SAINT ELISABETH ROSE OF CHELLES

SAINT ELISABETH ROSE OF CHELLES

(+1130)

FEAST DAY: 13 DECEMBER

Saint Elisabeth Rose of Chelles is known to have become a hermit and survived thanks to wild berries (hence the choice of her to bless this recipe). She began life as Rosa Villechausson, the daughter of a French noble, and soon entered the famed Benedictine Chelles Abbey near Paris. But her love of solitude was such that she obtained leave to retire and went to live in the hollow of a huge oak in the forest of Château-Landon, south of Fontainebleau. Mocked at first, in time she attracted some women to join her and together they founded the monastery of Sainte-Marie du Rozoy in nearby Courtenay (Loiret). Several years after her death, her body was disinterred and found to be incorrupt – a sign of her holiness (but perhaps also thanks to the wild berries?).

The statue that inspired this depiction of her shows her as an elegant nun with rosary beads in her hand.

Photographs: Douglas Freer; Maria Medvedeva / Shutterstock

SUMMER PUDDING

1. Put the berries in a saucepan. Add the sugar. Bring to a simmer over a low heat and cook for 3–5 minutes until the sugar has dissolved. Add sugar to taste, if needed – there should be a good balance between tart and sweet.
2. Line a 1 litre/1¾ pint pudding basin with clingfilm. Put the bowl on a piece of bread and cut around the base to make a round. Put the round of bread in the bottom of the bowl.
3. Line the inside of the bowl with more slices of bread, overlapping slightly to avoid any gaps. Spoon in the fruit, making sure the juice soaks into the bread. Reserve a few spoonfuls of juice.
4. Cut a slice of bread to fit the top of the pudding neatly, using a sharp knife to trim any excess from around the edges. Wrap in clingfilm, weigh down with a saucer and a tin can, and chill overnight.
5. To serve, unwrap the outer clingfilm, turn out the pudding onto a plate and remove the inner clingfilm. Drizzle over the reserved juice to cover any remaining white bread and serve with crème fraîche, if liked.

800g/1lb 12oz mixed summer berries, such as blackcurrants, strawberries and raspberries
125g/4½oz golden caster sugar
9 thick slices slightly stale white bread, crusts removed
crème fraîche or cream, to serve (optional)

Serves 6–8
Preparation: 20 minutes, plus 8 hours' chilling
Cooking: 6–8 minutes

SAINT GUÉNOLÉ

SAINT GUÉNOLÉ (+532)
FEAST DAY: 3 MARCH

Brittany in France is home to apple cider, so a saint from there is appropriate to bless this recipe: Saint Guénolé was the son of Fragan, a prince who fled from Cornwall with his wife Gwen, called the Three-Breasted (Teirbronn) as she had to feed triplets – all future saints. Guénolé (Winwaloe in Breton) was one of the three. He was brought by his father to be educated by Saint Budoc, a hermit-scholar living on the island of Lavret, one of a group of islands off the north coast of Brittany. Eventually Guénolé started a monastery on another island, Tibidy, near Brest, but this was such an inhospitable place the monks moved to nearby Landevennnec. The abbey founded there grew and became famous for centuries until it was destroyed at the time of the French Revolution; only ruins remain. Devotion to Saint Guénolé is still strong among the apple farmers, who believe he introduced the apple tree to Brittany.

This deptiction of Saint Guénolé illustrated here shows, by the saint's left hand side, the carved head of an angel and a branch with apples.

APPLE PUDDING

1. Preheat the oven to 180°C/350°F/Gas 4. Grease an ovenproof dish.
2. Peel, core and slice the apples in layers into the prepared dish, sprinkling each layer with demerara sugar and lemon rind.
3. Cream the caster sugar and butter together until pale and fluffy. Add the vanilla extract and the eggs and beat in very gradually, adding a little flour if the mixture looks like curdling.
4. Fold in the remaining flour and spread the sponge mixture evenly over the fruit. Bake in the preheated oven for 35–40 minutes until well-risen and golden brown. The pudding is cooked when a skewer inserted into the centre of the sponge topping comes out clean.
5. Dredge with caster sugar and serve hot with custard.

450g/1lb cooking apples

85g/3oz demerara sugar

finely grated rind of 1 lemon

100g/3½oz caster sugar, plus extra for dredging

100g/3½oz butter or margarine, plus extra for greasing

1 tsp vanilla extract

2 eggs, beaten

100g/3½oz self-raising flour

custard or cream, to serve

Serves 6
Preparation: 20 minutes
Cooking: 35–40 minutes

Variation:
You could add some blackberries to the apple layers, or substitute sliced pears for the apples. In season, use gooseberries, rhubarb with grated orange rind, or halved plums or apricots.

SAINT IGNATIUS

SAINT IGNATIUS OF LOYOLA (+1556)
FEAST DAY: 31 JULY

The link between this recipe and Saint Ignatius is not immediately obvious: oranges are not associated with the Basque country where Ignatius (then called Iñigo) was born in 1491. However there is a phrase in his Spiritual Exercises which provides a clue. He includes there 'Rules by which to perceive and understand to some extent the various movements produced in the soul'. With great sensitivity he notes, 'When souls are advancing from good to better, the touch of the good angel is soft, light and gentle, like a drop of water making its way into a sponge. The touch of the evil angel is rough, accompanied by noise and disturbance, like a drop of water falling on a stone' (Exx 335). Ignatius may not have had in mind the subject of our recipe, but the word 'sponge' provides a link, and our hope is that those who partake of this sponge will indeed be 'advancing from good to better'.

Saint Ignatius writing the Spiritual Exercises. This painting, which hangs in the hall of the novitiate in Harborne, Birmingham, is a copy of the original version (1950) in the Sacred Heart Church, Wimbledon, London.

RECIPE
ORANGE SPONGE

Tip:
A soft dropping
consistency has
been achieved when
the mixture falls off
the wooden spoon
by the time you
count to five.

1. Grease a 850 ml/1½ pint pudding basin. Use a fine grater to remove the rind from the orange, avoiding the pith, then peel off all the pith. Reserve the rind. Cut the orange into horizontal slices, on a plate to catch the juice. Reserve the juice.
2. Spread the golden syrup over the base of the prepared basin and arrange the orange slices on it.
3. Cream the butter and sugar with the reserved rind until pale and fluffy. Whisk the eggs with a fork and add them, 1 tablespoon at a time, beating well between each addition. If the mixture begins to curdle, add a spoon of the flour each time you add some egg.
4. Sift the flour and baking powder together and fold quickly and lightly into the mixture.
5. Add the reserved orange juice and mix in enough of the water to produce a soft dropping consistency. Spoon the mixture into the basin on top of the orange slices. Cover with greased foil and put into a steamer.
6. Cover and cook for 1½ hours, or until a skewer inserted into the centre of the pudding comes out clean. Remove the pudding from the pan and leave to shrink slightly before turning out onto a warmed platter.
7. Serve with the orange-flavoured custard.

1 orange
2 tbsp golden syrup
100g/3½oz butter or margarine, plus extra for greasing
100g/3½oz caster sugar
2 eggs
100g/3½oz plain flour
2 tsp baking powder
1–2 tbsp lukewarm water
orange-flavoured custard, to serve

Serves 6
Preparation: 20 mins
Cooking: 1½ hours

SAINT

SAINT RICHARD

SAINT RICHARD (+1266)
FEAST DAY: 30 DECEMBER

The Saint Richard remembered for this recipe, although English by birth, became a monk in a Cistercian monastery in Aduard, in the province of Groningen in the northern Netherlands. He is also known as Richard de Busto, which may indicate that he came from Buxton in Derbyshire – which is the county where the Bakewell Tart was invented. After studying in Paris he went to the Holy Land on pilgrimage and was instructed by a female hermit gifted with clairvoyance that he should become a Cistercian in Frisia (a place he had never heard of). When, shortly afterwards, Richard met three noblemen from Frisia, he saw it as a sign. He entered the abbey of Aduard and, being a learned man, became the head of the monastic school. He was also very devout, and was known to work miracles while he himself was suffering greatly from various ailments. Shortly after his death his relics were placed in the altar and he was revered. The expense of official canonisation was excessive, but the order declared him a saint. The illustration depicts Saint Richard at work in the infirmary.

ICED BAKEWELL TART

1. To make the pastry, place the flour and salt in a bowl and rub in the butter and vegetable fat until the mixture resembles breadcrumbs. Alternatively, blend quickly in a food processor in short pulses. Add the eggs with sufficient water to make a soft, pliable dough. Knead lightly on a board dusted with flour, then chill in the refrigerator for about 30 minutes. Roll out the pastry and use to line a 23 cm/9 inch loose-based tart tin. Meanwhile, preheat the oven to 180°C/350°F/Gas 4.
2. To make the filling, mix together the butter, sugar, almonds and eggs and add a few drops of almond extract. Spread the base of the pastry case with the jam and spoon over the filling.
3. Bake in the preheated oven for about 30 minutes, or until the filling is firm and golden brown. Remove from the oven and leave to cool completely.
4. When the tart is cold make the icing by mixing together the sugar and lemon juice, a little at a time, until smooth and spreadable. Spread the icing over the tart, leave to set for 2–3 minutes and sprinkle with flaked almonds. Chill in the refrigerator for about 10 minutes before serving.

Serves 6–8
Preparation: 25–30 minutes, plus 40 minutes' chilling
Cooking: 30 minutes, plus cooling

Rich pastry
175g/6oz plain flour, plus extra for dusting
pinch of salt
60g/2¼oz butter, cut into small pieces
55g/2oz white vegetable fat, cut into small pieces
2 small eggs yolks, beaten

Filling
125g/4½oz butter, melted
125g/4½oz caster sugar
125g/4½oz ground almonds
2 large eggs, beaten
few drops of almond extract
2 tbsp seedless raspberry jam

Icing
125g/4½oz icing sugar, sifted
6–8 tsp fresh lemon juice
25g/1oz toasted flaked almonds

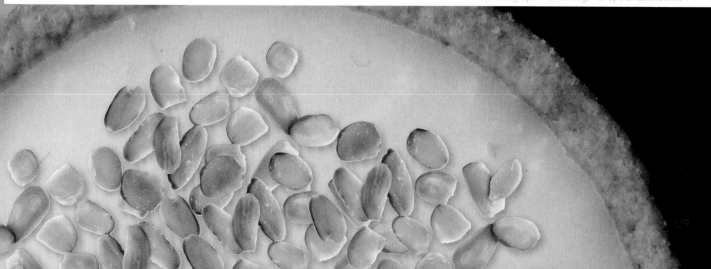

SAINT
SAINT ROBERT OF CÎTEAUX

SAINT ROBERT OF CÎTEAUX (+1110)
FEAST DAY: 29 APRIL

The choice of Saint Robert of Cîteaux for this recipe was an easy one. The story goes that on one occasion he was called to assist the ailing Duchess of Bar-sur-Seine and she told him that what she most wanted was a plate of strawberries. It was winter and there was snow on the ground, but Saint Robert dug under the snow and, sure enough, found the strawberries she wanted. At the time of the story he was probably abbot of the Abbey of Cîteaux near Dijon, which he helped to found.

Before his birth, his mother had a dream in which Our Lady handed her a ring, saying that it was for the son to be born. At the age of fifteen, Robert entered a Benedictine abbey, but soon felt the need for reform and, together with some companions, founded a new monastery at Molesme in Burgundy, so that he is also known as Saint Robert of Molesme. Both abbeys were part of the reform movement within the Benedictine tradition seeking greater austerity and simplicity. The Cistercians, as they came to be called, shunned decoration in their churches, all dedicated to Our Lady, and followed a severely penitential daily timetable.

STRAWBERRY MERINGUE ROULADE

1. Preheat the oven to 220°C/425°F/Gas 7. Lightly grease a 23 x 33 cm /9 x 13 inch Swiss roll tin cover base with lining (baking) paper.
2. Whisk the egg whites until stiff peaks hold. Add the sugar, 1 teaspoon at a time, and continue to whisk until all the sugar has been incorporated and the mixture is stiff and glossy.
3. Spoon the meringue into the prepared tin and tilt to level the surface. Sprinkle over the flaked almonds.
4. Bake near the top of the preheated oven for about 8 minutes until the top is golden brown.
5. Reduce the oven temperature to 160°C/325°F/Gas 3 and bake for a further 10 minutes, or until the meringue is firm to the touch.
6. Remove the meringue from the oven and turn out onto a fresh sheet of baking paper. Peel the lining paper from the base and leave the meringue to cool for 10 minutes.
7. Spread the whipped cream evenly over the meringue, and scatter the strawberries over the cream.
8. Roll up the meringue from a long end, using the fresh sheet of baking paper to help lift it. Wrap the roulade in more baking paper and leave to chill in the refrigerator for about 30 minutes. Lightly dust with icing sugar before serving.

vegetable oil, for greasing
4 egg whites
250g/9oz caster sugar
40g/1½oz flaked almonds
300ml/10fl oz double cream, whipped until thick
250g/9oz strawberries, sliced
sifted icing sugar, for dusting

Serves 8
Preparation: 30 minutes
Cooking: 18 minutes, plus 40 minutes' cooling and chilling

Photograph: Shalith / Shutterstock

SAINT RUADAN

SAINT RUADAN (+6TH CENTURY)
FEAST DAY: 30 AUGUST

If Saint Ruadan was true to his Irish name (rua = red or red-haired), he would have had ginger hair, and so would be an appropriate patron for this recipe. Unfortunately, little is known about him, although he seems to have been a hermit living in the woods near Tavistock in Devon. He is said to have founded several churches in Cornwall, where he was known as St Rumon (or Ruan).

STEAMED GINGER & CINNAMON SYRUP PUDDING

1. Bring a large saucepan of water to the boil. Meanwhile, lightly grease a 600 ml/1 pint pudding basin. Put the golden syrup into the bowl.
2. Cream together the butter and sugar until pale and fluffy. Gradually beat in the eggs until the mixture is glossy. Sift the dry ingredients together and fold into the mixture with the ginger. Add the milk to make a dropping consistency.
3. Spoon the batter into the prepared basin and smooth the top. Cover with a pleated piece of greaseproof paper to allow for expansion. Tie with string and steam for 1½–2 hours, topping up the water level as required.
4. Turn out onto a plate to serve.

3 tbsp golden syrup

125g/4¼oz softened butter, plus extra for greasing

115g/4oz caster

3 eggs, lightly beaten

115g/4oz plain flour

1 tsp baking powder

1 tsp ground cinnamon

25g/1oz stem ginger, finely chopped

2 tbsp milk

Serves 4
Preparation: 20 minutes
Cooking: 1½-2 hours

The Christmas tree in the dining room at Manresa, December 2018. Framed photo: Simon Bishop SJ, director of novitiates. Dries van den Akker SJ, author of the lives of the saints; Colette Scully and Martina Maher, authors.

CHRISTMAS

SAINT BRIGID OF KILDARE

SAINT BRIGID OF KILDARE, PATRON OF IRELAND (+523)
FEAST DAY: 1 FEBRUARY

Saint Brigid is venerated in Ireland as a patron both of the island (along with Saint Patrick) and of poultry, including turkey. The monastery of Kildare, where both men and women were included, was founded by Brigid and ruled by her as abbess. Earlier the locals had venerated a pagan goddess called Brighde, and (thanks to her medieval biographer, Cogitosus) various miracles connect the two, Saint Brigid being famed as a *thaumaturga* (miracle worker). Her touch made the trees (including the evergreen Christmas tree) flourish, and the curious legend arose that she had been present at the birth of Christ in Bethlehem. This may have some connection with the fact that some knights from Bruges in Flanders brought relics of Saint Brigid to Belém (the word for Bethlehem in Portuguese), so she (or her relics) were said to be in Bethlehem.

HEAVENLY ROAST TURKEY

1. Preheat the oven to 220°C/400°F/Gas 7. Loosen the skin over the turkey breast by slipping your fingers between the flesh and skin at the neck end, leaving the skin attached at the cavity end. Spread butter over the breast under the skin. Slip a few lemon slices and thyme sprigs under the skin.

2. Stuff the neck end of the turkey up to the breast with the stuffing. Use any leftovers to make stuffing balls to roast around the bird – never put meat stuffing in the main cavity as this is not safe. Secure the loose skin with skewers, or just tuck the skin under. Fill the body cavity with the remaining lemon slices, herbs and the onion. Tie the legs together with string to give a neat shape and lightly butter the skin.

3. Arrange two sheets of foil across a large roasting tin: they must be large enough to go over the breast. Place the turkey on top and fold the sheets of foil over the turkey, leaving a large air gap between the turkey and foil.

4. Cook the turkey in the preheated oven for 40 minutes, then reduce the oven temperature to 160°C/300°F/Gas 3, and roast for a further 3½ hours, basting occasionally.

5. Increase the oven temperature to 220°C/400°F/Gas 7. Take the turkey out of the oven, turn back the foil and drain most of the juice from the tin into a jug or bowl and set aside. Baste the bird with any juices remaining in the pan and return to the oven, uncovered, for 30 minutes.

6. Pierce the thickest part of the thigh with a sharp knife. If the juices are clear the turkey is cooked – cover with the foil and a thick towel and leave to stand for 30 minutes before carving. If the juices are still tinged pink, roast for a little longer. Serve with all the trimmings.

1 x 6kg/13lb oven-ready turkey

115g/4oz butter, softened

1 lemon, thinly sliced

3 small fresh thyme sprigs

½ quantity Lemon and Thyme Pork Stuffing (see page 141)

1 onion, cut into wedges

Serves 12–15
Preparation: 20 minutes
Cooking: 4 hours 40 minutes, plus 30 minutes' standing

SAINT WENCESLAS

SAINT WENCESLAS (+935)
FEAST DAY: 28 SEPTEMBER

It may seem disrespectful to link Saint Wenceslas with a recipe for gravy, but there are good reasons: firstly, Christmas brings memories of the carol:

> Good King Wenceslas looked out
> On the feast of Stephen
> When the snow lay round about
> Deep and crisp and even.

And, secondly, as the carol reminds us, goodness appears when one accompanies: Wenceslas gave strength to his page as he went with him:

> In his master's steps he trod
> Where the snow lay dinted
> Heat was in the very sod
> Which the saint had printed.

And it is the function of gravy to accompany and assist.

Unfortunately goodness often attracts envy and Wenceslas, who was Duke of Bohemia, was assassinated (probably by his brother, Boleslas the Cruel).

RECIPE

CHRISTMAS TURKEY GRAVY

1. After pouring off the turkey juices into a bowl or jug, let the fat rise to the top. Place 2 tablespoons of the fat in the tin in which you roasted the bird. Spoon off the remaining fat in the bowl or jug and set aside, reserving the juices.
2. Place the tin over a medium heat, add the flour and cook for 1 minute, stirring and scraping the sediment from the tin. Gradually pour in the stock and port, whisking. Add the jelly, bring to the boil, then simmer for 2–3 minutes.
3. Add the turkey juices, season, strain and serve.

Tip:
Don't discard any turkey fat. Any that isn't used can be put in the fridge and used for roast potatoes at a later date.

roasting juices from your turkey
25g/1oz plain flour
600ml/1 pint giblet stock
150 ml/5fl oz port
2 tbsp redcurrant jelly
salt and freshly ground black pepper

Serves 8
Preparation: 5 minutes
Cooking: 3–6 minutes

SAINT BLAISE OF SEBASTE

SAINT BLAISE, BISHOP (+316)
FEAST DAY: 3 FEBRUARY

Saint Blaise is said, while on his way to a martyr's death, to have cured a child who had a fish bone stuck in his throat. He is well known because of the blessing of throats with two crossed candles given in his name in many churches. However, another story links him to the pork which figures in this recipe. A very poor widow lost her only possession, a pig, to a ravenous wolf. She asked Blaise for help and, sure enough, the pig was duly returned by the obedient wolf. When Blaise was imprisoned before his execution, the thoughtful lady brought him a dish with the head and paws of the pig. Her kindness is mirrored by that of the two ladies who have prepared these recipes.

LEMON & THYME PORK STUFFING

1. Melt the butter in a saucepan, add the onion and cook gently for about 10 minutes, or until softened.
2. Stir in the remaining ingredients and mix well, then set aside and leave to cool.
3. This is now ready to stuff the neck end of the turkey.

25g/1oz butter
1 small onion, chopped
450g/1lb pork sausage meat
55g/2oz fresh white breadcrumbs
juice and finely grated zest of ½ large lemon
2 tbsp chopped fresh parsley
leaves from 3 fresh thyme sprigs
salt and freshly ground black pepper

Serves 6–8
Preparation: 10 minutes
Cooking: 10 minutes, plus cooling

SAINT BENEDICT

**SAINT BENEDICT OF NURSIA
PATRON OF EUROPE (+547)
FEAST DAY: 11 JULY**

The great founder of western monasticism, Saint Benedict, suffered grievously from temptations against chastity while living as a hermit near Subiaco. Chastity and chestnuts are linked not simply by the sound of the two words but also by a certain symbolism: they are surrounded by thorns but survive. In the case of Benedict, he is said to have overcome the temptations by throwing himself into a thorn bush, as depicted in the illustration. Severity seems to have been a trait of his character, and when he was asked to become abbot of the monastery of Vicovaro, his rule displeased the monks so much that they tried to poison him. Leaving Subiaco, Benedict moved to Monte Cassino. Fortunately he learned moderation, as is clear from the famous rule he wrote for his monks to live a life of silence and prayer. This became standard throughout Europe, and Pope Paul VI proclaimed him the patron saint of Europe.

APRICOT & CHESTNUT STUFFING

1. Preheat the oven to 190ºC/350°F/Gas 5. Grease a 20 x 28 x 5 cm /8 x11 x 2 inch ovenproof dish.
2. Chop the apricots into raisin-sized pieces.
3. Put the water into a saucepan, add the onion and the apricots, bring to the boil and boil for 5 minutes. Drain well.
4. Put the breadcrumbs into a bowl. Melt the butter in a frying pan and pour half onto the breadcrumbs.
5. Add the chestnuts to the butter remaining in the pan and brown lightly. Mix with the apricots, sultanas, onion, cranberries, parsley and breadcrumbs. Season well with salt and pepper.
6. Turn into the prepared dish and bake in the preheated oven for about 30 minutes until crisp.

225g/8oz ready-to-eat dried apricots
600ml/1 pint water
1 large onion, roughly chopped
225g/8oz fresh white breadcrumbs
85g/3oz cranberries
85g/3oz butter, plus extra for greasing
225g/8oz frozen chestnuts, thawed and roughly chopped
85g/3oz sultanas
large bunch fresh parsley, chopped
salt and freshly ground black pepper

Serves 6
Preparation: 20 minutes
Cooking: 30 minutes

MARTYR
ANTONIO CRIMINALI SJ

ANTONIO CRIMINALI (+1549)
FEAST DAY: 18 MAY

For this recipe, the servant of God and martyr Antonio Criminali is chosen for an odd reason: the word 'sizzling' in the recipe recalls the name of the place where he was born, Sissa, near Parma in Italy. Antonio joined the Jesuits shortly after they were founded and was sent to India in 1545 to join Saint Francis Xavier who sent him to Cape Comorin in the south of India. While staying at Vedâli, a group of Hindu pilgrims, enraged by a Portuguese tax on worship at the great shrine at Rameswaram, attacked the mission and Antonio was killed.

Antonio is shown clearly identified to the left of Saint Francis Xavier.

SIZZLING SAUSAGES IN BACON

1. Preheat the oven to 190°C/375°F/Gas 5. Stretch out each of the rashers with the back of a knife and cut each one into three pieces.
2. Wrap a piece of bacon tightly around each sausage, and place, spaced well apart, on a baking tray.
3. Cook in the preheated oven for 45 minutes, or until cooked through and crisp. Serve hot with roast turkey.

6 rashers dry-cured streaky bacon
18 cocktail sausages

Serves 6
Preparation: 15 minutes
Cooking: 45 minutes

SAINT ARNIKIUS OF AVERBODE

SAINT ARNIKIUS OF AVERBODE (+1208)
FEAST DAY: 17 MARCH

There is a curious link between Saint Arnikius of Averbode and berries. Somewhat of a legendary figure, Arnikius is said to have been of noble stock. After a pilgrimage to the Holy Land he became a monk in the Norbertine Abbey of Averbode. He was given permission to live as a hermit in the forest. One day he was in his cell when a poor woman came to pick berries. She left her baby in the shade of a tree but was horrified when a wolf suddenly appeared and picked up the child. When he heard her screams Arnikius rushed out and ordered the wolf to drop the baby at once, which it did. There were teeth marks on the baby, but they disappeared at a kiss from Arnikius.

SPECIAL CRANBERRY SAUCE

1. Place all the ingredients in a shallow saucepan and stir to combine.
2. Bring to the boil over a medium heat, then reduce the heat and simmer gently for 10–15 minutes, stirring occasionally. Serve warm.

Tip:
Don't worry if the sauce looks a bit runny at the end of the cooking time – it will thicken when it cools.

450g/1lb fresh or frozen
   cranberries
225g/8oz caster sugar
juice and finely grated zest
   of 1 orange
3½ tbsp port
3½ tbsp cider vinegar
large pinch of ground allspice
large pinch of ground cinnamon

Serves 20
Preparation: 10 minutes
Cooking: 10–15 minutes

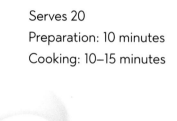

Photographs: Zigzag Mountain
Art: Richard Griffin / Shutterstock

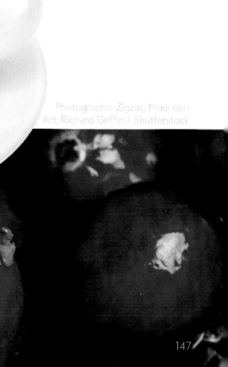

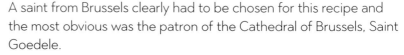

SAINT GOEDELE (GUDULA)

SAINT GOEDELE (+712)
FEAST DAY: 8 JANUARY

A saint from Brussels clearly had to be chosen for this recipe and the most obvious was the patron of the Cathedral of Brussels, Saint Goedele.

In medieval Latin, her name, Gudula, means 'good girl'. Brought up by an aunt, who lived as a hermit, she came home to lead a pious life in the city of Brussels. Every morning, at cock crow, she would go to mass carrying a lantern, but on one occasion the lantern went out and Goedele feared she would be lost. So she prayed and the lantern lit of its own accord, allowing her to fulfil the command of the Lord, 'See that you have your lamps lit' (Luke 12:35), but perhaps mainly to show us the need to have the light of the Lord to guide our steps.

BUTTERED BRUSSELS SPROUTS

1. Bring a saucepan of lightly salted water to the boil. Meanwhile, prepare the sprouts, removing the outer leaves. Trim the base, and cut a cross in the base of each sprout.
2. Cook in the boiling water for 5–6 minutes, depending on size, until just done – don't overcook!
3. Drain, toss in the butter, season with salt and pepper to taste and serve immediately.

900g/2lb Brussels sprouts
25g/1oz butter
salt and freshly ground black
   pepper

Serves 8
Preparation: 20 minutes
Cooking: 5–6 minutes

SYRO-PHOENICIAN WOMAN

Both Matthew (15:21ff) and Mark (7:24ff) record a passing reference of Jesus to bread and crumbs, which links an anonymous Syro-Phoenician woman to this recipe. It reveals a remarkable person admired by the Lord. She is mentioned when Jesus sets out for the territory of Tyre. Although he wanted to remain incognito, a woman, whose little daughter had an unclean spirit, heard about him and came and fell at his feet. She is not named, but Mark says that she was a gentile, not a Jew, and by birth a Syro-Phoenician, so not an Israelite. When she asks Jesus for help, he replies rather rudely, 'The children should be fed first, because it is not fair to take the children's bread and throw it to the dogs.' She is not put off and replies warmly, 'Ah, yes, sir, even the dogs under the table eat the children's crumbs!' Perhaps Jesus was a little ashamed that he had been so curt, or was he just testing her? In any case, he said to her, 'Great is your faith! Let it be done for you as you wish.' Sure enough, she went home, found the child lying on the bed, the demon gone. And like this woman (if not thanks to her!) all those who are gentiles can partake of the bread of the Lord.

© Peter Clare. 2000. Private Collection

In the modern painting one can recognise the mother with her child, and the dogs being pointed out by Jesus.

BREAD SAUCE

Tip:
To avoid waste, the onion could be cut up finely and used in stuffing

1. Stud the onion with the cloves and put into a saucepan with the bay leaves and milk. Bring to the boil, remove from the heat, cover and leave to cool for at least 15 minutes.
2. Remove the onion and bay leaves from the pan with a slotted spoon, discarding the bay leaf.
3. Add the breadcrumbs to the milk and bring to the boil, stirring. Simmer for 1–2 minutes.
4. Stir in the cream and butter, then add salt and pepper and nutmeg to taste. Serve hot.

1 onion, peeled and left whole

8 cloves

2 bay leaves

450ml/16 fl oz milk

100g/3½oz fresh white breadcrumbs

150ml/5fl oz double cream

25g/1oz butter

pinch of freshly grated nutmeg or ground cinnamon

salt and freshly ground black pepper

Serves 8
Preparation: 15 minutes
Cooking: 20 minutes, plus cooling

Photograph: Magnago / Shutterstock

SAINT MOSES

SAINT MOSES
FEAST DAY: 4 SEPTEMBER

The choice of Saint Moses as a patron for this recipe is accidental in more ways than one. This pudding should be served with a good sprinkling of brandy which is set alight: the sprig of holly placed on top may well catch fire, and remind us of the burning bush seen by Moses.

> Moses was keeping the flock of his father-in-law Jethro, the priest of Midian; he led his flock beyond the wilderness, and came to Horeb, the mountain of God. There the angel of the Lord appeared to him in a flame of fire out of a bush; he looked, and the bush was blazing, yet it was not consumed.
> (Exodus 3:1–2)

Moses removed his shoes (as can be seen in the illustration) and approached and was able to speak with God who declared his name: I AM who I AM (Exodus 3:14). The art of the Eastern Churches has depicted this revelation as a prophecy of Christmas, when God would declare his name once more in the arms of Mary, who is burning with the love of God but not consumed.

Photograph: Monkey Business Images / Shutterstock

CHRISTMAS PUDDING

Tip:
This pudding should be made at least six weeks before Christmas

1. Lightly grease a 1.4 litre/2½ pint pudding basin. Cut out a small square of foil and press it into the base of the basin. Put the dried fruit and apple into a mixing bowl with the orange juice. Add the brandy and leave to soak for about 1 hour.
2. Using an electric mixer cream the butter, sugar and orange rind until pale and fluffy. Gradually beat in the eggs, adding a little flour; don't worry if it curdles.
3. Sift together the flour and mixed spice, then fold into the creamed mixture with the breadcrumbs and almonds, if using. Add the dried fruit with the apple and the soaking liquid and stir well.
4. Spoon into the prepared basin, press down and level with the back of a spoon. Cover the basin with a layer of greaseproof paper and a layer of foil, both pleated across the middle to allow for expansion. Tie under the lip of the basin with string and trim off the excess paper and foil.
5. Put the pudding in the top of a steamer filled with simmering water, cover and steam for about 8 hours, topping up the water as necessary. Remove from the steamer and leave to cool completely. Discard the paper and foil, make holes in the pudding with a fine skewer and pour in a little more brandy or rum to feed. Cover with fresh paper and foil. Store in a cool, dry place.
6. To reheat on Christmas morning, put the pudding basin in a steamer filled with simmering water and simmer for 3 hours.
7. To serve, pour some some brandy over the pudding. Set alight, then serve with brandy butter.

450g/1lb dried fruit
40g/1½oz currants (optional)
1 small cooking apple, peeled, cored and roughly chopped
juice and grated rind of 1 orange
3½ tbsp brandy or rum, plus extra for feeding
85g/3 oz butter, softened, plus extra for greasing
100g/3½oz light muscovado sugar
2 eggs
100g/3½oz self-raising flour
1 level tsp ground mixed spice
40g/1½oz fresh white breadcrumbs
40g/1½oz whole shelled almonds, roughly chopped (optional)
brandy and Brandy Butter (see below), to serve

Serves 8–10
Preparation: 45 minutes, plus 1 hour's soaking
Cooking: 8 hours + 3 hours

BRANDY BUTTER

1. Measure the butter into a bowl.
2. Beat well with a wooden spoon until soft – or use an electric hand mixer.
3. Beat in the icing sugar, then add the brandy. Spoon into a dish, cover and keep in a cool place until needed.

225g/8oz unsalted butter, softened
450g/1lb icing sifted icing sugar
3–5 tbsp brandy

Serves 8–12
Preparation: 15–20 minutes

THREE KINGS

**THE MAGI: BALTHAZAR, MELCHIOR
AND CASPAR (+1ST CENTURY)
FEAST DAY: 6 JANUARY**

This recipe can be served during the Christmas celebrations, and thus a link is provided to the Three Kings, or the Magi, as Matthew (2:1–12), the only evangelist to mention them, prefers to call them. Originally they may have been intended to recall the words of Psalm 72:10: 'May the kings of Tarshish and of the isles render him tribute, may the kings of Sheba and Seba bring gifts.' It is not surprising that very soon these 'wise men' were venerated as kings and even given ages (20, 40, 60) and names (Balthazar, Melchior and Caspar). They were seen as representing the three continents of the known world: Africa, Europe and Asia. Their number (three) was deduced from the number of their gifts, but it is reasonable to imagine that among their gifts there were also dishes of food.

SHERRY TRIFLE

1. Spread the trifle sponges with jam, then cut them into bite-sized cubes and arrange in the base of a large glass serving bowl. Pour over the sherry and leave to stand for 30 minutes.
2. Combine the raspberries and strawberries and spoon them over the sponges.
3. To make the custard, put the egg yolks and sugar into a bowl and whisk together. Pour the milk into a saucepan and heat gently over a low heat. Remove from the heat and gradually stir into the egg mixture, then return the mixture to the pan and stir constantly over a low heat until thickened. Do not boil.
4. Remove from the heat, pour into a bowl and stir in the vanilla extract. Leave to cool for 1 hour. Spread the custard over the trifle, cover with clingfilm and chill in the refrigerator for 2 hours.
5. To make the topping, whip the cream in a bowl and stir in the sugar to taste. Spread the cream over the trifle, then scatter over the chocolate pieces. Chill in the refrigerator for 30 minutes before serving.

Serves 4–6

Preparation: 20 minutes, plus 30 minutes' standing

Cooking: 5–20 minutes, plus 3½ hours' cooling and chilling

100g/3½oz trifle sponges
raspberry jam, for spreading
150ml/5fl oz sherry
150g/5½oz frozen raspberries, thawed
350g/12oz fresh strawberries, sliced

Custard
6 egg yolks
50g/1¾oz caster sugar
500ml/18fl oz milk
1 tsp vanilla extract

Topping
300ml/10fl oz double cream
1–2 tbsp caster sugar
1 chocolate bar, crumbled

SHEPHERDS AT THE BIRTH OF CHRIST

SAINT LUKE TELLS US ABOUT THE SHEPHERDS WHO WERE THE FIRST TO COME AND ADORE THE NEWBORN CHRIST

'In the countryside close by there were shepherds out in the fields keeping guard over their sheep during the watches of the night. An angel of the Lord stood over them and ... the angel said, "Do not be afraid ... Today in the town of David a Saviour has been born to you; he is Christ the Lord." ... Now it happened that when the angels had gone from them into heaven, the shepherds said to one another, "Let us go to Bethlehem and see this event which the Lord has made known to us." So they hurried away and found Mary and Joseph, and the baby lying in the manger ... And the shepherds went back glorifying and praising God for all they had heard and seen, just as they had been told.' (Luke 2: 8–20)

Luke says nothing of their gifts, but left artists – and us – to imagine; perhaps the shepherd to the right of baby Jesus has a cake in the basket he holds.

 Photograph: Christopher Elwell / Shutterstock

CHRISTMAS CAKE

Tip:
Make this
cake at least
three weeks in
advance

1. Put all the dried fruit into a bowl and pour over the brandy. Cover and leave to soak overnight.
2. Preheat the oven to 110°C/ 225°F/Gas ¼. Grease a 20- m/8 inch cake tin and line with baking paper. Cream the butter and the sugar in a bowl until pale and fluffy. Gradually beat in the eggs. Stir in the orange and lemon rind and treacle.
3. Sift the flour, salt, baking powder and mixed spice into a separate bowl, then fold into the egg mixture. Fold in the soaked fruit and brandy, almonds and hazelnuts, then spoon the mixture into the prepared tin. Make a small hole in the middle of the cake. This is to give a flat top to your cake.
4. Bake in the preheated oven for at least 3 hours. If the cake is browning too quickly, cover with foil. The cake is cooked when a skewer inserted into the centre comes out clean. Remove from the oven and leave to cool on a wire rack overnight. Store in an airtight container until required.
5. To ice the cake, roll out the marzipan and cut to shape to cover the top and sides of the cake. Brush the cake with the jam and press the marzipan onto the surface.
6. Put the egg whites into a bowl and add the icing sugar a little at a time, beating well until the icing is very thick and will stand up in peaks. Spread over the covered cake, using a fork to give texture.
7. Decorate with silver dragées and ribbon.

Variation:
You can replace
the nuts with an
extra 55g/2oz
dried fruit of
your choice.

1175g/6oz raisins

125g/4½oz currants

125g/4½oz sultanas

100g/3½oz glacé cherries, rinsed

150ml/5fl oz brandy

225g/8oz butter, plus extra for greasing

200g/7oz soft dark brown sugar

4 eggs, beaten

grated rind of 1 orange

grated rind of 1 lemon

1 tbsp black treacle

225g/8oz plain flour

½ tsp salt

½ tsp baking powder

1 tsp mixed spice

25g/1oz chopped toasted almonds

25g/1oz chopped toasted hazelnuts

Icing

750g/1lb 10oz marzipan

3 tbsp apricot jam, warmed

3 egg whites

650g/1lb 7oz icing sugar

silver dragées and ribbon, to decorate

Makes 1 x 20-cm/8-inch cake
Preparation: 40 minutes, plus overnight soaking
Cooking: 3 hours, plus cooling

ALPHABETICAL LIST NAMES OF SAINTS

11.01*A biblical person who doesn't have a feast day in the calendar of saints and is therefore celebrated on All Saints Day, which is intended for such cases!

CALENDAR OF SAINTS

11.01*A biblical person who doesn't have a feast day in the calendar of saints and is therefore celebrated on All Saints Day, which is intended for such cases!